# How to Drink Natural Wine

# How to Drink Natural Wine

Rachel Signer

MITCHELL BEAZLEY

# CONTENTS

6 Introduction

## 1
## WHAT IS NATURAL WINE?

- 12 When the Old is New: A Pre-Modern Approach
- 16 Defining the Undefinable: What Is Natural Wine?
- 18 Beaujolais Beginnings: The New Naturalists
- 22 A Natural Phenomenon: Natural Wine's Rise
- 24 The Republic of Georgia: Millennia of Natural Wine
- 28 Natural Wine Styles to Know
- 36 Icons: Producers to Try
- 60 Expert View: Inside the Natural Wine World
- 64 DOCs, AOCs, Etc: What Three Letters Can Mean for a Wine
- 66 Is Natural Wine Vegan?
- 68 What's in a Name? Different Ways to Talk About Natural Wine

## 2
## FROM GRAPE TO GLASS

- 72 The Dirt on Organics & Biodynamics
- 78 Maria Thun's Biodynamic Lunar Calendar
- 80 Natural Vinification: From Juice to the Bottle, Featuring Wild Yeasts
- 96 Stages of Natural Vinification
- 100 The Art of Fermentation: A Personal Anecdote
- 102 You Say Grapes, We Say Biodiversity: A Naturalist Understanding of Vine-Growing
- 106 Bubbles, Naturally
- 110 Expert View: What's the Big Deal with Sulfites?
- 114 What Is Terroir? And What Does Natural Wine Have to Do with It?
- 118 Chaos Theory Meets Natural Wine: A Conversation with Austrian Wine-Growers Gut Oggau

# 3
## CHOOSING, POURING, ENJOYING

124 A No-Rules Culture
126 Decoding a Natural Wine Label
130 We've Got the Funk: Tasting & Describing Natural Wines
136 Natural Wine & Potential Flaws
140 What to Do If a Wine Is Flawed
142 Serving Temperatures & Decanting
146 Aging & Storing Natural Wines
148 Expert View: The Art of Pairing Natural Wines with Food
154 Perfect Pairings You Must Try
156 Not So Good: Pairings to Avoid
158 Hosting a Natural Wine-Forward Gathering

# 4
## GOING DEEPER

186 Destination Natural Wine Bars
188 Natural Wine Fairs Around the World
194 A Harvest Experience: What to Know
198 Visits & Tastings: Etiquette & a Form for Taking Notes
204 Getting into a Natural Wine Career
208 Expert View: "Oops, I Became a Winemaker"
212 Oh, the Wine-Soaked Places You'll Go

216 Further Reading
218 Index
222 About the Author & Acknowledgments

# INTRODUCTION

I REMEMBER MY FIRST GLASS of natural wine. It was like that moment in *The Wizard of Oz* when the film suddenly turns to color. The world lit up with the liveliness on my palate. "What is that?" I wondered, with my nose plunged into a glass of Gamay that smelled of crushed roses, freshly plowed fields, and something truly wild. I was desperate to know more.

Ten years later, I've been a wine salesperson, wine journalist, wine educator, and winemaker, always in the "natural" realm, and I'm here to share my experience with you. Natural wine is a vast subject that takes us around the world—from the Republic of Georgia and northeast France's Loire Valley, to the hills of Tuscany, the mountains of Lebanon, and the Australian countryside. As with art, you could study natural wine your entire life and still have questions left unanswered.

With infinite growing and making styles in the world of natural wine, it is impossible to learn them all from a book; for a deeper understanding, you'd have to spend time in vineyards and wineries. However, *How to Drink Natural Wine* lays out the basic knowledge you need to continue exploring natural wine on your own. It is truly a privilege to be able to dedicate any part of one's life, whether a full-time career or a hobby, to understanding natural wine. The pursuit will take you to breathtakingly gorgeous farms, the stylish wine bars of Tokyo and Copenhagen, and sweaty or freezing-cold tastings where you'll slosh glasses with strangers who become your friends.

Welcome to the journey. Pour yourself a glass of something nice, and let's dive in.

# WHAT IS NATURAL WINE?

# WHEN THE OLD IS NEW: A PRE-MODERN APPROACH

In the past ten years, a grassroots movement has taken hold in the global wine industry. "Natural wine"—sometimes called "low-intervention," "raw," or "pure" wine—is often easy to spot in a glass. First, there's the cloudy appearance. Often the color, too, appears brighter, more luminescent. It is also found in surroundings that don't look like the serious enotecas of the past: A natural wine bar might have a state-of-the-art turntable sound system and serve expensive oysters, but there's no dress code, and the glassware is simple all-purpose.

The idiosyncrasies of natural wine are numerous, but for its devotees, natural wine is the truest expression of terroir, that intersection of place, climate, and people that is at the heart of wine culture.

Natural wine is a self-defined and decentralized category that is both old and new. On the one hand, it's been practiced continuously for millennia in the Republic of Georgia, where evidence of grape fermentation in clay amphorae goes back to 6000 BCE. The ancient civilization that came to be known as the Etruscans migrated to the Italian peninsula from the East, bringing with them *Vitis vinifera*—the subspecies we know today as wine grapes—which they trained up trees, a beautiful practice known as *vite maritata* that is continued even today. Ancient Romans documented the Etruscans using wine in their rituals and ceremonies, highlighting its importance in their culture and cosmology.

There were no machines for harvesting and crushing grapes back then, no enological additives to be found, with the exception of sulfur dioxide, which could be harvested from volcanic sites. Wine wasn't a commodity; it was a liquid expression of culture. Even when wine did become a commercial item—with estates making barrels exclusively for imperial kings and delivering vats to cities for commoners to enjoy in taverns—glass bottles were scarce until the 20th century, so you wouldn't have been able to walk into a shop and grab something for home.

Up until the 20th century, fermented grape juice was a drink that was, contradictorily, both very elitist and part of a peasant's way of life. Across the Mediterranean region, it was common for families and neighborhoods to have grapevines trellised above their gardens.

They would take the grapes to a cooperative-run wine press to make wine to drink at home. Meanwhile, Champagne was famously the drink of the czars, and Hungarian sweet wines were beloved by European kings.

Things changed dramatically for wine with greater availability of glass for bottles, and inventions such as stainless steel (1912) and the automated bottling line (1959), as well as the introduction of tractors for mechanized grape harvesting (from the 1950s onward). These technical innovations, along with population growth, conspired to convert wine into a middle-class drink, something affordable for the masses. This is cause for both celebration ("Yay, we all get to enjoy wine!") and concern ("Hmm, there's a lot of absolute plonk out there"). In the face of this mass production—as well as a certain hype for manipulated wines that came about in the 1980s—natural wine strives to recall the pre-modern era when wine was a handmade, farmed drink that communicated culture and history.

Like most movements, natural wine exists on a spectrum. At the extreme end, we have wine made exclusively without any sulfites or filtration, while at the other end there are low-intervention wines made with some filtration and "minimal" sulfite additions, and perhaps even some temperature control in hot regions. Many natural winemakers do use modern machines such as the pneumatic press and automated bottling lines, and materials such as stainless steel and fiberglass are extremely common in natural wineries.

Despite these variations, the movement's unifying ethos is rooted in a non-commercial, anti-chemical approach as well as an independent, anti-corporate spirit. It's a return to the peasant roots of winemaking, with a touch of postmodern aesthetics and playfulness. The fact that natural winemakers don't all agree on how things should be done is an indication of the movement's philosophical, radical nature. Natural wine isn't here to be defined, it's for producers to express their farming and creativity as best they can, while respecting an increasingly challenging, rapidly changing climate, and with the aim of delivering stable, drinkable wines to the market. Each producer has their own vision and approach.

But with all the wine out there—and the ability of corporate wineries to mimic the natural wine aesthetic—how can we know if a wine is actually "natural"? What do we even mean by "natural"? And when, and from where, did this movement emerge?

# DEFINING THE UNDEFINABLE: WHAT IS NATURAL WINE?

There is no simple definition or certification for "natural wine," and different individuals, communities, and events have divergent opinions on what natural wine is or should be. That said, generally speaking, most definitions would assume some or all of the following:

* Vineyards farmed organically* (including biodynamically), meaning without pesticides, fungicides, or herbicides
* Hand-harvested grapes (versus machine-harvested)
* Wines made without commercial yeasts or acids/colorants, or any of the other dozens of enological inputs permitted in conventional winemaking
* Unfiltered (or lightly, non-chemically filtered) and unfined wines
* "Minimal"** or zero sulfite additions
* Made by an independent entity—that is, not from a corporate winery
* Ethically made—that is, workers being treated and paid fairly

\* Note that (1) organic farming does allow the use of copper and sulfur to protect vines from disease; (2) some organic and biodynamic wineries are certified and will indicate this on the label, while others are not, for administrative or ideological reasons.

\*\* There's no agreed-upon quantity that defines "minimal" sulfite additions, with some events and certifications permitting a maximum of 50ppm (**parts per million**) of added sulfites, an amount that some would say is quite high. Many people assert that a wine is only considered natural when zero sulfites are added, while others consider this approach extreme. See p. 111 for a detailed discussion of sulfites.

---

**Parts per million:** A unit of measurement that expresses the amount of a substance in a larger mixture; 1ppm = 1mg per liter.

# BEAUJOLAIS BEGINNINGS: THE NEW NATURALISTS

France, the 1980s: Architect I M Pei is working on the glass pyramid at the entrance to the Louvre. Gérard Depardieu is cementing his burgeoning career starring in the notable film *Jean de Florette*. Paris is buzzing with one of the world's best nightlife scenes and the pared-back yet elegant dining of the nouvelle cuisine movement.

Even in the French countryside, cultural change was afoot—especially in Beaujolais. This historic wine region was well known for its signature **grape variety**—Gamay. A light and crunchy red, Gamay grew throughout Beaujolais's slopes and steep, granite hills.

Despite a prevalence of wonderful terroir in the region, Beaujolais producers were struggling on the market. Their wines were considered inferior to those of other regions in France, largely because so many of them belonged to the "Nouveau" category—wines released only two months after harvest, to be consumed immediately. To meet the market's demands, Beaujolais winemakers practiced chaptalization, whereby sugar is added during fermentation to boost the alcohol content, for a boozy, simple young wine. On top of this, winemakers had begun resorting to commercial yeasts and heavy doses of sulfites to stabilize their rapidly bottled Nouveau wines.

There were bigger problems—all over France: Since World War II, chemical pesticides, herbicides, and fungicides were increasingly common in viticulture and agriculture. The idea was to boost production as much as possible.

Wine, once an integral part of life, had become heavily commercialized. It was a dead product. The vignerons of Beaujolais, tired of their wines being viewed as low quality, began to experiment with sulfite-free winemaking, gradually leading to a revolution. Two central figures included a chemist named Jules Chauvet, who began attempting zero-sulfite-added wine in the 1950s, and a young winemaking student called Jacques Néauport, who helped spread the gospel of organic farming

**Grape variety:** A named cultivar of grapevine. Note that the term "varietal" should not be used in this sense and instead refers to a wine made of one variety. Grape varieties in this book are capitalized for emphasis.

# decades later, natural wine is being produced in every corner of the world

and natural winemaking among Beaujolais growers. Thanks to Chauvet and Néauport, a group of Beaujolais winemakers known affectionately as the "Gang of Four" (though some accounts suggest there were five or more in this loose collective) began making natural wines. One of these producers, Marcel Lapierre, was particularly influential; winemakers elsewhere in France often attribute their first attempts at natural wine to a memorable encounter with Lapierre.

Over time, word spread of the Beaujolais Gang of Four as their bottles proved popular in the bistros of Paris, such as Belleville's Le Baratin, still an incredible dining experience to this day. The wines even impressed drinkers overseas, thanks to their importer, the famed Kermit Lynch, and his ally Alice Waters, chef-owner of Chez Panisse in Berkeley, California. Among producers, the Gang of Four's influence fanned out over other French regions, as well as Italy and Spain. Decades later, natural wine is being produced in every corner of the world—from Oregon's Willamette Valley to Chile's Itata and Australia's Adelaide Hills—and there's a new cohort of naturalists in Beaujolais, too.

Of course, there were always producers who simply never modernized and made natural wine by default throughout the decades. But the Gang of Four helped spawn a fresh generation of winemakers who valued organic farming and wanted to make the purest wine possible, without any additives.

# A NATURAL PHENOMENON: NATURAL WINE'S RISE

Why has natural wine's influence ballooned from the bistros of Paris to taking over the wine bars of New York City and Los Angeles, blanketing the fine-dining restaurants of Copenhagen, and peppering the streets of Tokyo, Sydney, and Montréal?

In New York City from around 2007 to 2010, early adopters like The Ten Bells and Uva Wines grew followings for their natural wine offerings. Additionally, synth-pop band LCD Soundsystem, who had enjoyed natural wines on their European tours, helped spread its popularity when back in the city. Across the country, San Francisco had Terroir and Ruby, both focused on natural wines; Oakland's Ordinaire and Domaine LA in Los Angeles were also instrumental on the scene. In 2009, Terroirs wine bar opened in London, celebrating natural wines. In Australian cultural capitals Sydney and Melbourne, a cluster of new natural wine festivals and bars popped up from 2010 onward.

In 2015, LCD Soundsystem frontman James Murphy, with three partners, opened restaurant and wine bar The Four Horsemen in the Williamsburg neighborhood of Brooklyn. The Four Horsemen was an immediate success and is still a massively popular destination for

# supporting organic farming is one way that everyday consumers can make a difference

natural wine, having picked up the James Beard Award for Outstanding Wine Program in 2022.

It's not always professional "wine people" who embrace natural wine. Often, the opposite is true: These organic, wild-fermented unfiltered wines seem to attract people from a range of backgrounds who never otherwise thought a wine passion was for them.

There's another factor, too: Younger generations of drinkers are aware that the planet's temperatures are rising. Supporting organic farming is one way that everyday consumers can make a difference. It may seem like a drop in the bucket to drink a natural wine when the climate is changing so rapidly, but the Food and Agriculture Organization of the United Nations states that "Organic agriculture not only enables ecosystems to better adjust to the effects of climate change but also offers major potential to reduce the emissions of greenhouse gases."* It even suggests that organic farming may counteract climate change by "restoring the organic matter content" of soil by promoting soil resilience to "water stress and nutrient loss," and through **carbon sequestration**.

Wine drinkers are choosing to support organic growers, preferring to pour from a bottle that was made with the least amount of environmental damage. We can also thank farmers' markets for the revolution in our kitchens—even when it comes to wine. My mother has always maintained that my interest in natural wine is directly connected to the fact that she grew pesticide-free tomatoes and corn every summer in our backyard. Could it be that eating organic, farm-fresh food primes our palate for natural wines? All of this is why natural wine is not, as some would say, just a trend—it's a rising tide.

\* `Organic Agriculture, Environment and Food Security,` Nadia El-Hage Scialabba & Caroline Hattam (2002).

**Carbon sequestration:** This is when carbon dioxide from the atmosphere is captured and stored, the goal being to mitigate the effects of climate change.

# THE REPUBLIC OF GEORGIA: MILLENNIA OF NATURAL WINE

**One of the world's most unusual wine cultures is also its oldest—and it is a hotbed of natural wine.**

The Republic of Georgia, in central Eurasia, is considered the longest continuously producing wine country in the world and the home of the ***Vitis vinifera*** grapevine. Remains of amphorae—clay vessels used for fermentation—dating back to 6000 BCE, the Neolithic period, have been found in Georgia. Despite this being a time of hunter-gatherer culture, the Georgians made the effort to harvest grapes and ferment them in handmade clay vessels.

Over time, those vessels—known as *qvevri*—remained important in Georgian winemaking. Remarkably, they are installed underground, which permits fermentation or aging to happen in a cool, dark environment. Georgian winemakers traditionally put full grape clusters into amphorae for extended macerations, resulting in strongly perfumed and flavored orange wines.

In the 20th century, Georgian culture was suppressed by 70 years of Soviet occupation. In all the Soviet territories, agriculture—including viticulture—became forcibly state-owned. What this meant for Georgian wine was severe regulation of its production: Four varieties were permitted for growing (Rkatsiteli, Mtsvane, Tsolikouri, and Saperavi) out of the five-hundred-plus varieties found throughout the country. With some exceptions, wine was produced in bulk, without regard for origin, and largely for consumption in Moscow.

Growers were permitted to keep their vineyards of non-sanctioned varieties alive in very limited sizes, and they were allowed to vinify them for home consumption, which by default meant natural winemaking. This wasn't a trend; it was simply the way things had always been done: Modernization came with the Soviets. When Georgia became independent in 1991, the country slowly began to re-embrace its incredible, historic winemaking heritage.

---

***Vitis vinifera***: The species of grapevine that was domesticated and naturalized over time in Europe and elsewhere and from which most of the world's wine is made; *Vitis vinifera* is one of dozens of species of the genus *Vitis*.

Word eventually spread that Georgian wines were worth exploring—for their incredible diversity, as well as for their natural production, including fermentation in the underground *qvevri*. Producers around the world—notably in the Friuli region of Italy—began requesting *qvevri* for their wineries, eager to try out this ancient method, and you can now find *qvevri*-made wine from the Loire Valley, Sicily, and California.

Today, Georgian natural wines can be enjoyed around the world: Producers such as Iago's Wine and father/daughter team Archil and Nino Guniava are making gorgeous blends and single-variety wines fermented with skin contact in *qvevri* as their ancestors would have done for thousands of years. Bottlings from incomers like Pheasant's Tears (see p. 55) and Ének Peterson, who fell in with Georgian terroir, are also easily found abroad. While the four Soviet varieties are the most commonly produced, there is fortunately still a wealth of viticultural diversity in Georgia that makes it an irresistible place to explore for anyone interested in natural wines.

The influence of Georgian winemaking has spanned the world, even reaching the Momento Mori winery in Australia, where amphora are used for skin-contact whites. While this isn't a Georgian *qvevri* per se, it holds similar benefits in terms of temperature control and neutrality.

# NATURAL WINE STYLES TO KNOW

We are lucky to be able to find an incredible selection of handmade natural wines in nearly any major city these days. For those just discovering the category, the array of offerings can be daunting: The styles, flavors, and labels of natural wines are unquestionably very different from those of conventional wines.

Think of natural wine exploration like learning a new language: grasping a fresh lexicon of terms related to farming and fermenting. It's an exhilarating path to walk down—and once you're on it, seduced by the unpredictable, romantic world of these earthy, handcrafted wines, there's no turning back. The list below contains some of the styles you might encounter in your naturalist explorations.

## ORANGE WINE (SKIN-CONTACT OR MACERATED WHITE WINE)

This wine is made from white grapes with maceration, or soaking, on their skins, which leads to a yellow or orange hue. It is a white wine made in the style of a red. What we normally think of as white wine results from the immediate pressing of yellow/orange-skinned grapes that have white juice. If you delay pressing and allow the grapes to soak with their skins, the color and flavor of the skins seep into the juice. Not all orange wines are natural, but within the natural wine arena, skin-contact white wine is an important category, because the wines deliver exceptional flavor and are versatile with food.

# PÉT-NAT (*PÉTILLANT-NATUREL*)

Originally French, this additive-free way to produce a sparkling wine has since gone global. Instead of dosing a dry wine with sugar and yeasts for a second fermentation, producers simply bottle a wine at a precise moment before it has **fermented dry**. The sugar within converts to carbon dioxide, and what you get is a fizzy wine. After some aging, the wine goes through a laborious **disgorgement** process, resulting in an extremely elegant sparkling wine. Try pét-nat with your starter platter of meats and cheeses, or nibbly food like arancini, anchovy soldiers, crudités, or fried chicken. The term "ancestral method" is also applied to this style.

**Fermented dry:** When we say that a wine has fermented dry, it means that all the sugars have been converted into alcohol. There is no detectable residual sugar.

**Disgorgement:** This is the releasing of the excess tartrates (crystalline deposits of potassium bitartrate that form in wine during fermentation and aging) and lees that have accumulated in a carbonated wine, then replacing that volume with new wine and resealing with a crown cap or cork.

## COL FONDO & REFERMENTED-IN-BOTTLE

At some point, you've no doubt enjoyed a glass of Prosecco, which is a sparkling wine from the Veneto region of northern Italy, made from the Glera grape variety and using the Charmat method (see p. 107). Its natural cousin is *col fondo*, a traditional method of making fizzy white wine from Glera. *Col fondo* is made by bottling a wine while provoking a secondary fermentation by adding frozen grape must, allowing carbon dioxide to form in the bottle. *Col fondo* wines are not filtered or disgorged; they are aged on their **lees** and delightfully cloudy, resulting in a satisfying texture that makes for a pleasant, stand-alone starter drink. This refermented-in-bottle approach, though it doesn't have a catchy name, is a popular way of making naturally sparkling wine outside of northern Italy, too.

**Lees: Deposits of spent yeast and other particles that settle at the bottom of a vat or bottle of wine.**

Natural Wine Styles to Know

## GLOU GLOU

This French term refers to highly drinkable bottles that tend to disappear within 20 minutes of opening. Usually a red and low in alcohol, this is something you'd serve chilled without food, on a patio with friends. (*Above.*)

## PIQUETTE

Once a by-product of winemaking made for harvest workers, this very low-alcohol style has seen a recent comeback. It's made by taking just-pressed grapes and pouring water over them to coax out the last bit of fermentation. Canned piquette is a picnic treat.

## BLENDS

By far the most common form of a natural wine is an ambiguous blend whose composition would surprise you if you were privy to it. Pinot Gris and Gamay—two French varieties not typically associated with each other? Why not. Dark-red Alicante Bouschet with a touch of the Italian white variety Garganega? Could be! Unconfined by appellation rules, tradition, or market constraints, natural winemakers are free to play around with blending varieties that historically weren't vinified together. Winemakers also love to bottle what are known as field blends, meaning they harvest an old vineyard where numerous, often obscure varieties are co-planted, then ferment it as one wine: reds, whites, pink-skinned varieties—whatever happens to grow there—all mixed together.

# GROWER CHAMPAGNE

In terms of production, there are two kinds of Champagne: that made by growers, and that made by houses. "Grower Champagne" refers to Champagne made primarily or exclusively from estate-owned vineyards, while Champagne houses make wines from purchased grapes or leased vineyards. You can find codes on Champagne labels that break this down for you: RM (*récoltant-manipulant*) is a grower; NM (*négociant-manipulant*) is a house.

Growers tend to be smaller in scale because they're limited to what they possess, while houses can produce hundreds of thousands of bottles annually from vineyards around the region. A grower brand is usually family-owned, while a house may be part of a larger, corporate conglomerate. Yes, like that ubiquitous yellow label you're thinking of—though it would be an error to assume that all Champagne houses are as commercial. Some are quite artisanal; they simply don't own the vineyards and so get classified as a house. Another distinction is that growers are more terroir-focused, since they can bottle or blend according to vineyard location or soil type.

A grower Champagne can be a thing of striking beauty, with years of aging and finessed bubbles mingling with careful attention to terroir. Are all grower Champagnes natural? Not necessarily. When it comes to making Champagne from organic or biodynamic vineyards, the already small pool of grower Champagnes narrows; and when you restrict it even further to grower Champagnes made with minimal sulfites and/or minimal *dosage*, it becomes a mere handful of names. *Dosage* in this context is a particular kind of additive that is fundamental to the traditional method; it is added after disgorgement but before the final aging, and consists of a mixture of yeast and sugar. What to consider is that some Champagnes are zero *dosage*, which means they have used fresh grape juice as an alternative to the sugar/yeast concoction—this delivers great purity in the sparkling wine. Meanwhile, some producers use higher-quality sugar, or simply less of it, in their *dosage*.

When your criteria for grower Champagnes include being made entirely without added sulfites, the options are paltry, but look for two producers in the Côte des Bar region: Rupper-Leroy works almost entirely without sulfites, and Marie-Courtin makes one gorgeous sulfite-free Champagne called Concordonce. It's worth noting that there are also houses that farm biodynamically and organically, such as Louis Roederer. Variation in the Champagne region is infinite.

Natural Wine Styles to Know

# ICONS: PRODUCERS TO TRY

Once dismissed as a fleeting trend, natural wine is clearly here to stay. Increasingly, independent producers around the world are dedicating themselves to organic viticulture and additive-free, minimalist fermentations.

While it's always fun to explore new labels, here are some of the most iconic natural winemakers to try while you're educating your palate. It was difficult to curate this list given the plethora of wonderful natural winemakers out there, so as much as possible, I used the following criteria:

* They have at least 12 vintages (or close to it) under their belts
* They have consistently and uncompromisingly made natural wine over the years
* They have had a notable influence on the natural wine community as a whole
* Their wines are reasonably available worldwide

# EUROPE

## SPAIN

**ORIOL ARTIGAS:** Part of the younger generation that has benefited from figureheads in Spanish natural wine such as Joan Ramón Escoda and Laureano Serres, after more than a decade it's clear that Oriol Artigas is one of Catalonia's most talented wine producers. Oriol's wines are based on high-elevation, coastal vineyards in the region of Alella, just outside Barcelona, including whites based on one grape, Pansa Blanca, an ancestor of Xarel·lo. The depth of flavor, acidity, and texture in these wines only improve with age.

**PARTIDA CREUS:** This much-loved project, founded by two Italian architects-turned-winemakers, has been producing wine from old, abandoned vineyards around Catalonia since 2007. Their no-sulfite offerings tend to be rustic, lively, and unforgettable. The pair also make an exceptionally tasty vermouth called Muz.

# FRANCE

**ANNE & JEAN-FRANÇOIS GANEVAT:** This biodynamically farmed Jura estate has seen ownership go back and forth in recent years, but the brother/sister duo continues to release bottlings of excellent quality. The Ganevats have a wonderful ***négociant*** range, but their estate wines are knockouts. Known for their mineral, saline profile, enhanced by long aging in barrels, the Ganevat wines display the uniqueness of Jura terroir.

**CHAMPAGNE BENOÎT LAHAYE:** A grower Champagne made with estate biodynamic vineyards (farmed with their own horse), oak aging, and zero ***dosage***. The gorgeous Violaine is made without any added sulfites whatsoever—extremely rare for the region.

*Négociant*: This French term describes winemakers who purchase fruit, as opposed to growing their own. Winemakers can be both estate-growers and *négociants*. Also abbreviated as *négoce*.

*Dosage*: This is a sugar mixture added to wines made in the traditional Champagne method.

**DOMAINE BINNER:** Christian Binner took over his family estate in Alsace in 1999 and has been making serious natural wines ever since, often with a touch of oxidation (see p. 137). He farms the typical Alsatian varieties—Riesling, Gewurztraminer, Pinot Gris, Muscat, and Pinot Noir—and makes his wines in an extraordinary winery designed according to **anthroposophic** principles.

**Anthroposophic:** Stemming from the overarching ideology of the anthroposophy movement helmed by Rudolf Steiner, of which biodynamic farming is one branch.

**DOMAINE DE L'ANGE VIN:** Jean-Pierre Robinot is a living legend who makes zero-addition wine with extensive aging in an old cave dug into a hillside, in the northern reaches of the Loire Valley, where Pineau d'Aunis and Chenin Blanc vines grow to 90 years old. Robinot was making natural wine very early on in the 2000s, after a career running a bistro and wine journal in Paris. Robinot's sparkling wine Les Années Folles, named for the "crazy years" of France in the 1920s, is a real treat, and the wild Pineau d'Aunis and slightly oxidative Chenin wines are ethereal experiences.

**DOMAINE DE L'OCTAVIN:** Alice Bouvot has been farming and making natural wine in the Jura since 2004 under the label Domaine de l'Octavin. These zero-sulfite-added wines from biodynamically farmed vineyards are an excellent introduction to this fascinating, cool-climate French region. Bouvot also makes wine from vineyards elsewhere in France, because of low yields in the Jura in recent years. L'Octavin wines can be racy and ebullient, or slightly more structured, depending on the **cuvée**.

**Cuvée: This word has various meanings in wine production, but in this book it is used to refer to a type, blend, or batch of bottled wine.**

**DOMAINE MOSSE:** The Mosse family is an excellent representation of the eclectic, creative vibe of Loire Valley natural wine culture. This northwestern cool-climate region in France, marked by the presence of the Loire River, is a notable hotbed of natural wine where an unusaul diversity of grape varieties results in endless combinations of playful blends. With vineyards the family manages around the Anjou region, the Mosses make particularly good Chenin Blanc for aging, various red blends, and a fantastic sparkling rosé called Moussamoussettes.

**MATASSA:** Originally from South Africa, Tom Lubbe settled in southern France and began carefully farming old vineyards for making skin-contact whites and ethereal light reds. Each bottle is an experience you hold onto. Cuvée Marguerite—a vivacious, succulent skin-contact blend of Macabeu, Muscat d'Alexandrie, and Muscat à Petit Grains—is one of my all-time favorite wines.

**MAISON PIERRE OVERNOY:** Hang out in natural wine circles long enough, and you're bound to hear this name, though you'll be lucky if you ever try a bottle from this famed Jura estate. Pierre Overnoy is credited as having one of the original natural wineries; he had the impulse to stop using sulfites back in the 1980s and is also known to have begun the practice of topping-up barrels (***ouillé***) at a time when the Jura was known for an oxidative approach. His protégé Emmanuel Houillon has been the winemaker here for some time. Beautiful, simple red and white wines, originally bottled in 50cl size but now in the standard 75cl, these are extremely limited in quantities and much coveted.

*Ouillé*: Known as ullage in English, this term refers to the head space that occurs when wine has evaporated from a barrel during the aging process. Someone who makes *ouillé*-style wines is topping up, or replacing, the ullage with fresh wine, thus preventing oxidation.

## GERMANY

**RITA & RUDOLF TROSSEN:** Farming their estate biodynamically since the late 1970s and working without sulfites since 2010, the Trossens make unfiltered, unfined, zero-additive German wines—and they are exceptionally drinkable and age-worthy. If you're a fan of Riesling, Trossen wines are for you: They make several expressions with this German white-variety hero.

## AUSTRIA

**CHRISTIAN TSCHIDA:** The Burgenland region is home to many notable natural winemakers—including Gut Oggau, another icon, which is featured on p. 118. With his first release in 2000, Christian Tschida brought the world's attention to this region; he makes racy, low-alcohol, no-sulfite-added wines from 14 hectares (35 acres) of vines that have been in his family for generations. With higher prices and limited quantities, these seductive wines have achieved cult status worldwide.

**STROHMEIER:** The Austrian region of Styria is home to a cluster of natural winemakers, including Franz Strohmeier. With impressive bottles featuring a spiral shape on the label and a delicate paper seal over the cork, Strohmeier wines showcase the minerality of Styrian terroir through mysterious blends. Franz is known as something of a renegade in his viticultural approach; he likes to experiment with unpruned vines, edging them toward their wild side. His naturalism and curiosity come through in the wines.

# ITALY

**DENAVOLO:** In the Piacenza hills of Emilia-Romagna, winemaker Giulio Armani moonlights at Denavolo after his day job of making wine at famed natural wine estate La Stoppa. The Denavolo project works with local grape varieties such as Ortrugo and produces some of the most sapid, delightful skin-contact whites out there.

**FORADORI:** Elisabetta Foradori's estate in the Dolomites has steadfastly embraced native varieties like Teroldego and Manzoni Bianco while farming biodynamically and fermenting in amphorae, with a significant percentage of **whole-bunch**. Wines receive sulfite additions generally at bottling. Lezèr, a light red made from Teroldego, came into being when hailstorms damaged fruit in 2017, but it has stuck around and is now one of the estate's more approachable wines.

Whole-bunch: Grape clusters (or bunches) still on their stems—as in, not destemmed.

**NINO BARRACO:** The area surrounding the city of Marsala, in western Sicily, was mostly known for fortified wines until a few estates began looking for Marsala terroir in traditional, dry winemaking. Since his first vintage in 2009, Nino Barraco has been quietly making some of Sicily's most captivating wines, while experimenting relentlessly with forgotten and underappreciated native grapes. His white blends and Grillo varietal display the sea-breeze minerality of Marsala's coastal vineyards, and his age-worthy Zibibbo wine is complex and layered. Barraco's *rosato* (rosé) of local red varieties is saline, tart, and inspiring.

**PĀCINA:** Custodians of a polycultural farm on the grounds of a 10th-century monastery that borders the Chianti Classico region in Tuscany, the multigenerational family behind Pācina is known worldwide for consistently gorgeous, meditative wines made with traditional local varieties. As well as vines, they grow *farro* (spelt), chickpeas, and lentils, and farm an olive grove for oil.

**VINO DI ANNA:** Mount Etna in Sicily is one of the world's most unusual wine regions, and this is perhaps one of its most unusual projects, founded in 2008 by Anna Martens and Eric Narioo, lifelong wine professionals. Vino di Anna is an ongoing exploration of the potential of Etna terroir, ranging from the rehabilitation and (limited) use of an old *palmento* (a type of ancient Sicilian structure specifically for winemaking), to the propagation of grapes mostly native to Etna (mainly Nerello Mascalese, Nerello Cappuccio, Carricante, and Grecanico) from old vineyards, and the installation of Georgian *qvevri* for fermenting wine.

**CANTINA GIARDINO:** One of the first natural wines I fell in love with was the Sophia, a well-macerated Greco wine from Cantina Giardino. For more than 20 years, husband-and-wife team Antonio Di Gruttola and Daniela De Gruttola have produced singular wines without sulfite additions, working with high-elevation vineyards in the Campania region. Cantina Giardino wines can be elegant or powerful, wild or slightly volatile—but they are always exciting and vibrant.

**OCCHIPINTI:** In the area of Vittoria in western Sicily, the Occhipinti family has been making waves with its wines for decades—beginning with the COS label, started by three friends, among them Giusto Occhipinti. His niece Arianna later founded this eponymous winery, stunning the world with her first vintages while she was only in her twenties. The lush, incredibly drinkable SP68 wines are perennial favorites in wine bars around the world: red and white blends of local Sicilian grapes, made in concrete.

## CZECHIA

**RADIKON:** The natural wine movement owes much to the region of Friuli-Venezia Giulia, close to the border with Slovenia, and one of our greatest debts is to the Radikon family. Stanko Radikon was one of the early innovators who showed the world the potential of the wines of northeastern Italy, which he did by going back to the traditional local approach of very extended maceration on white grapes and a natural, unfiltered, minimalist style. No natural wine exploration is complete without a bottle of Radikon.

**MILAN NESTAREC:** When you're bored of French wine, head to Moravia. The wines of Milan Nestarec include several ranges that run the gamut from playful (such as one-liter bottles with crown caps) to serious (the "white label" wines made from older vineyards). It's unusual to find such an exceptionally talented, thoughtful, and experimental winemaker whose bottlings are also approachable and endearing.

## GEORGIA

**PHEASANT'S TEARS:** John Wurdeman has been instrumental in reviving the natural wine culture of the Republic of Georgia, with deep reverence for tradition. The majority of Pheasant's Tears wines are made in underground *qvevri*, and over the years the winery has built a repertoire of offerings from rare, indigenous Georgian grapes. The amber-hued Rkatsiteli is a great introduction to Georgian wines; Pheasant's Tears make it with skin-contact, for an amber-hued wine, or in the cuveé pictured, without maceration.

## THE AMERICAS

**BICHI WINES:** In the Valle de Guadalupe, just south of the California border, 90 percent of Mexico's wine is produced. In this dry climate with sandy soils, the Bichi family farms 10 hectares (25 acres) biodynamically. Grape varieties include the famous colonial Mission grape, as well as others unique to Mexico. The Bichi wine range, first made in 2014, includes bright, energetic sparklings and unusual blends—it's what to serve to delight and surprise your jaded friend who thinks they've had all the natural wines out there.

**RUTH LEWANDOWSKI:** The winemaker is Evan rather than Ruth Lewandowski at this California project centered on single-vineyard wines from high-elevation, dry-farmed plots growing unusual varieties like Cortese and Grenache Gris. (Ruth is a reference to the Book of Ruth in the Old Testament, alluding to the cycle of death and life.) The enticing wines are a must-try when exploring the American genre, particularly the endearing Feints, a field blend full of crunchy-fruit texture underscored by brightness.

**LA GARAGISTA:** While the European grapevine *Vitis vinifera* usually gets all the accolades, Deirdre Heekin is elevating the status of humble New World hybrid grapes in her Vermont winery. Her wonderful experiment is a gift to us all—not only because the wines are so delicious and surprising but also because they open up the possibilities of what hybrid grapes can become. Don't miss her seductive sparkling cuvées.

## ELSEWHERE IN THE NEW WORLD

**LUCY M WINES:** One of the first natural wine labels in Australia—along with Jauma and Tom Shobbrook—Lucy M Wines,* under winemaker Anton van Klopper, offers surprising, edgy, and acidity-driven blends and **varietal wines**. They showcase cool-climate Adelaide Hills vineyards and never have any sulfites added. (*Left*.)

**TESTALONGA:** There's a thriving lo-fi wine scene in South Africa, and Craig and Carla Hawkins of Testalonga are leading their generation with their wines, particularly their vibrant skin-contact whites, including several made from Chenin Blanc. Every bottling is **single-variety**—so seek these out if you're a terroir nerd. (*Above*.)

**BEAU PAYSAGE:** Although it's challenging to find Japanese wines outside of the country itself, there is a flourishing natural wine movement there, and Beau Paysage is one of the more established standouts. In Japan's Yamanashi Prefecture, despite challenging humidity, Eishi Okamoto cultivates French varieties such as Merlot and Chardonnay. His handmade, limited-production Beau Paysage wines are known for their elegance and emotiveness and are a fascinating glimpse into Japanese terroir.

```
*   Full disclosure, I am the "other
half" of Lucy M Wines, so to speak.
```

**Varietal wines:** Made entirely from one variety of wine grape; a.k.a. "**single-variety**" or "**monovarietal**."

# EXPERT VIEW: INSIDE THE NATURAL WINE WORLD

## WITH ANIKA & CHRIS FOSTER OF ONLINE RETAILER MORE NATURAL WINE, BERLIN

Ten years ago, ordering natural wine online wasn't really a thing. MORE Natural Wine, a brick-and-mortar store in Berlin with a powerful online presence, has been one of the most visible changemakers in that space.

What sets MORE Natural Wine apart is not only the incredible inventory in their online shop but also their extensive trips to wine regions to interview producers about viticulture and winemaking practices. The online videos of these meetings serve as vital educational resources for consumers who want to better understand the wines they love.

Anika and Chris shared their story, highlighting the way that natural wines captured their passion and curiosity and created a new career path for them.

**HOW DID YOU WIND UP AS NATURAL WINE SELLERS?**
**CHRIS:** A few years back, Anika and I were running an entirely different business together. We'd tried a few natural wines and were curious about this genre when, one night, I was out to dinner and someone offered me a glass from a magnum [1.5-liter bottle] from then-unknown German producer Marto. It was his Weiss, a nondescript name meaning only "white."

I tried it and was forever changed—it was mind-blowingly good. Such a tropical bomb—pineapple, papaya, lychee, apricot, and vanilla—and only 10 percent alcohol. This was my moment of realization that you couldn't make a wine that tasted this way unless it was truly natural. I went home to Anika and declared my allegiance to the natural way, and then we started MORE Natural Wine.

**FOR PEOPLE JUST GETTING INTO NATURAL WINE, WHICH STYLE DO YOU RECOMMEND?**
**CHRIS:** When people are getting into natural wine, one thing I know will impress them is a *glou-glou* red. Something like Claus Preisinger's

# "okay, how are we gonna sell this and not freak people out?"

Puszta Libre—it's juicy and has very minimally invasive tannins. It's so popular that I think it should win awards for bringing people into natural wine. Including us.

Also, I'd recommend a low-tannin, orange wine. Really important about the tannins; we wouldn't push a strong orange wine from Georgia. To enjoy tannin, I'm a firm believer that you need to be already well on your natural wine journey.

Aromatic grapes like Gewurztraminer, when made with skin contact, are great. When made naturally they taste nothing like they do in the traditional wine world. People hear "Gewurztraminer" and they say, *Oh, I don't want a sweet wine*. But it's not—it's a floral, dry wine.

**ANIKA:** An example of this style is [Austrian biodynamic producer] Meinklang's Weisser Mulatschak, a skin-contact blend of Traminer, Pinot Gris, and Welschriesling.

**YOU DOVE INTO RUNNING A NATURAL WINE SHOP, BOTH BRICKS-AND-MORTAR AND ONLINE, WITH ZERO BACKGROUND IN WINE. ANY SURPRISES THERE?**

**CHRIS:** We were the first importer of Frauenpower [a wine made by Canadian Alanna LaGamba, in Germany; find an interview with her on p. 208]. What many people don't know is, one of the reasons it's called Frauenpower is because it was so explosive. The first one, the bar pressure was crazy—it just went everywhere. Alanna wasn't disgorging back then.

We didn't even know the words bar or pressure, but we thought, "Okay, how are we gonna sell this and not freak people out?" So we decided to focus on the "power" aspect of the name. Then Anika did this great video where she opens the bottle three different ways on the balcony. One of them, she puts into a ramen bowl and just kind of opens it and lets it go *whooooo* and drizzle down, and it fills up the ramen bowl, then she drinks it from a ladle. Another one was opening it with a saber, and another she just did it really slowly. That resonated with people.

**SOMETHING I'VE NOTICED IS THAT YOU KEEP TRAVELING TO THE JURA, AND YOU SEEM PARTICULARLY PASSIONATE ABOUT THAT REGION. HOW DID THAT COME ABOUT?**

**CHRIS:** We've drunk so much natural wine over the years, and you always try to find the crème de la crème. Maybe for conventional wine drinkers, that's Bordeaux or Burgundy. For people who want wines without added sulfites, because it's more alive, more of a real wine, there's nothing more exceptional than the huge amount of offering in Jura. Nearly every producer there in the natural wine world doesn't use sulfites, and the grapes are just captivating—Savagnin and Chardonnay with their acidity.

Jura winemakers are notable for their ability to make wine without sulfites because of the pH of the soil and the climate. People think natural wine is all dirty and funky, but the Jura is the top of the top in the wine world, where so many people are doing it naturally. I think it shows the elegance of the category.

**ANIKA:** Having fallen in love with Jura wines, we've also fallen in love with the people there. It's a stunning community. When we first went, there were open arms for us: We'd go into a cellar and have the best night, drinking incredible natural wines with producers. And it's also how they support each other. They've created this microcommunity, and it's so beautiful. They tell us stories about how they help each other and look out for each other—even the conventional winemakers. They're all there for each other. In other wine regions, that's not the case.

A good example is perhaps the most famous natural winemaker in the world, Pierre Overnoy. The number of times he's invited us into his home for tastings—but he and [his resident winemaker] Manu do that because they think it's the right thing to do for the wine community—to allow people to try older vintages. It's a surreal experience. The first time, it felt like the Three Kings visiting Jesus: the Italians there with gifts of Parmigiano, people from the Loire Valley with oysters. We used to bring homemade candles made out of bottles. You pay homage to the great.

# DOCs, AOCs, ETC: WHAT THREE LETTERS CAN MEAN FOR A WINE

Throughout this book, you'll see the above abbreviations mentioned in essentially one context: that nearly all the wines discussed are excluded from these categories. DOC and AOC refer to wine appellations in Europe that are intended to designate quality and tradition. And for various reasons, most natural wines are prohibited from inclusion, which affects their marketing.

We've discussed how, in the 20th century, European wine production was modernized and commercialized with chemicals and machines. At the same time, there was concern about the falsification of wines that were considered prestigious. In 1935, a French committee was created with the goal of determining *appellations d'origine contrôlée*—usually translated in

English as "controlled designations of origin"—to regulate and protect the production of French wine. The AOC concept was predicated on the notion of tradition: In order for a wine to belong to its local AOC, only certain vineyards, grape varieties, and quality levels would be permitted.

The first AOC created was the Arbois (Jura) appellation in 1936, and the system evolved over time to include more than 300 AOCs today. For wines that do not receive AOC status, various requirements and restrictions apply—for example, they may be prevented from including the grape varieties on a wine label, if these grapes are normally part of the appellation. Non-AOC wines in France would either be considered IGP (*indication géographique protégée*) or Vin de France ("wine of France").

Around the same time, Spain created its own appellation system. Other European nations followed suit. One commonality, no matter where, is that natural winemakers are often prohibited from inclusion in these appellations, regardless of the quality of their vineyards—for the simple fact that the wines taste different. Wild yeast fermentation, non-filtration, lack of sulfites—appellation tasting committees do not like these naturalist ways. The irony, of course, is that natural winemaking *is* the traditional way of these areas.

Being barred from the appellation (or choosing not to join, as some natural winemakers do) does have marketing consequences. It can affect sales abroad, for example. It also matters in terms of reaching consumers; many people have been taught that AOC or DOC means quality, and they turn their noses up at non-appellation wines.

It's fortunate that the global natural wine community has grown so much in the past three decades, because it ensures that a market exists for natural, non-appellation wines, which are known, not for a national certification of "quality," but rather for their pure expression of terroir—the confluence of place, culture, and climate.

New World wine regions—South Africa, Australia, the Americas, and so on—have also created appellations, but these are far less strict or impactful than the European ones and are generally considered mere geographic indicators.

# IS NATURAL WINE VEGAN?

This is one of the most frequently asked questions we receive in the industry. And it's one of the least straightforward to answer.

Many wines that would be categorized as either **artisanal** or conventional go through some form of "fining" process. To fine any liquid, including wine, an agent is added to the substance to precipitate excess solids, to make it easier to remove them. Common agents used in wine fining include casein (a milk protein), gelatin, isinglass (fish bladder protein), egg whites, and bentonite (clay). Of these fining agents, only clay would be considered vegan. Therefore, any wine that goes through fining is suspect in terms of being non-vegan.

It's rare for producers who profess to be part of the natural wine movement to be using fining agents—and if they use anything, it's generally bentonite. But nobody is required to mention fining on their label, so how do you know? The proof is usually in the pudding: When you see little bits of sediment swirling around in a freshly poured glass, it's unlikely that any fining took place.

However, it's not as simple as "all unfined wine is vegan." Biodynamic vineyards employ cow manure and other animal parts in fertilization. Some vineyards—organic or biodynamic—employ a workhorse. And many winemakers who do not fine at all do raise animals that they might use for fertilizer or as a food source.

Also worthy of consideration is that bees and insects will inevitably lose their lives during fermentation. Bees in particular are helplessly attracted to vats of freshly picked grapes and sometimes get lost in the crush. Of course, this is not intentional, nor is it unique to wine—in vegetable harvesting, too, insects lose their lives.

Vegans can be discerning as to which wines they are comfortable drinking by learning as much as possible about the production process from a trusted intermediary, such as an importer or salesperson.

---

**Artisanal:** In this book, artisanal wine refers to small-batch production that aims to be fine wine yet doesn't meet the definition of "natural" because of farming inputs or winery additives.

# WHAT'S IN A NAME? DIFFERENT WAYS TO TALK ABOUT NATURAL WINE

If you haven't had someone scoff at you when you say the phrase "natural wine," just keep saying it, and you will. And it could very likely be a winemaker.

Many people dislike the term "natural wine" and often reply that "all wine is natural." Some don't mind the phrase but prefer "living wine" or "pure wine" or "real wine." There are also "lo-fi wines" and "low-intervention winemaking." I've seen "naked wine" in print, but I haven't heard anyone casually throw it around at a party.

Often, winemakers comment that they don't appreciate the term "natural wine" because it seems exclusionary—they farm biodynamically but add 40ppm of sulfites and don't identify with their wines being "natural." It's understandable how the word could feel stifling to them.

We all wish that we didn't have to say "natural wine," which sounds by turns either clunky or smug, depending on the context, but we do so for a reason: to clarify that we are talking about wines made without conventional farming chemicals and without additives or mechanical intervention.

However, there's an interesting theory that the term "natural wine" is a misnomer, deriving from the original French phrase used to describe the Gang of Four's sulfite-free bottlings: *vin nature*. In French, to say that something is *nature* doesn't necessarily translate as "natural"; rather, it implies that it is in its purest form, with nothing added. Yogurt, for example, when sold unflavored in a French supermarket, is labeled *yaourt nature*. To take the phrase *vin nature* and make it into "natural wine" is not entirely correct, but translations rarely are. Instead, a translation is often an impression or a redefinition of the original concept. In this case, to say "nature wine" or "naked wine" or something a little closer to *vin nature* is awkward in English.*

The solution? Even as a writer, it stumps me. I stick with "natural wine" because I understand what it refers to. I also appreciate when people say, for example, "I prefer wines made from organic farms, with no additives"; that's very clear. Or if they said, "The restaurant has a list of low-intervention wines from small producers," I've got a good idea what would be on that list: maybe not the most extreme wines without sulfites, but probably some with minimal sulfites. Details can clarify things.

This eclectic, undefinable movement has been around for several decades, and somehow the phrase "natural wine" seems to come out on top again and again. Even so, it's perfectly valid if you prefer a different phrase.

```
*    Regarding the misnomer of vin
nature, other wine writers, including
Simon Woolf, have made this point
in their own work. See "How a False
Friend Created Natural Wine" (2025)
on Woolf's blog, The Morning Claret.
```

# the original French phrase used to describe the Gang of Four's sulfite-free bottlings: *vin nature*

What's in a Name?

# 2

# FROM GRAPE TO GLASS

# THE DIRT ON ORGANICS & BIODYNAMICS

**The artisanal nature of natural wine promises that each bottle or glass will be entirely unique. Every barrel and bottle is determined by the particularities of the vintage—namely weather but also the winemaker's ideas and decisions.**

Until the early 20th century, organics were the norm, everything was done by hand, and horses were used to plow vineyards. Now, though, we live in a modern world with a global market. It is a deliberate choice *not* to make "machine wine," a statement that rejects the treatment of wine as a commodity and draws a connection between human labor, nature's whims, and what we enjoy in a glass of pure, unadulterated living wine.

In artisanal winemaking, human hands are fully involved in the growing and picking of the grapes. Caring for vineyards is a year-round job, with important tasks ranging from winter pruning and regular weeding and mowing, to spraying the vines in spring at the start of the growing season to prevent disease. These sprays are where organic and non-organic diverse: Organic winemaking is based on the exclusion of certain inputs (sprays) broadly categorized as the triad of pesticides, fungicides, and herbicides.

In conventional, commercial viticulture (and agriculture), this triad is a cornerstone of machine-based farming, ensuring that nature and its pesky insects and invasive grasses stay out of the way. The goal is maximum production, even at the expense of long-term soil health. And there is, indeed, an expense to conventional farming.

Organic farming starts with the refusal of the triad of pesticides, herbicides, and fungicides. There are *some* organic-friendly versions of pesticides, but systemic chemicals are forbidden. Generally, organic farmers rely on what's known as a "Bordeaux mixture" of copper and sulfur to prevent the development of fungus, mold, and rot. Weeding, meanwhile, must be managed through diligent tilling or methods such as no-till and cover-crop growth.

## THE CONVENTIONAL FARMING TRIAD

Numerous studies have indicated the dangers of common chemicals used in the conventional farming triad.

Glyphosate—probably best known by the brand name Roundup—is the most concerning. Developed by Monsanto in the 1970s as a systemic herbicide that is applied topically (sprayed on) to plant foliage, glyphosate is marketed as a solution to problematic weeds and has become extremely popular in certain industries, such as soybeans. Seeds are now genetically engineered to be resistant to glyphosate so that farmers can spray an entire field without damaging crops.

In 2015, the World Health Organization declared that glyphosate causes cancer. Mice exposed to glyphosate show long-lasting damage to their brain, including Alzheimer's-like neurogenerative pathology.

Pesticides have been linked to Parkinson's disease among vineyard workers in studies by the University of California, Los Angeles, as well as the US National Institutes of Health.[*] In studies by the University of North Carolina at Chapel Hill, agricultural fungicides have also been shown to cause similar genetic changes in mouse neurons to those seen in autism and Alzheimer's disease.

Skeptics might claim that none of these chemicals is present at toxic levels in the actual wine that you drink. Regardless, vineyard workers are exposed to these substances, harming them and their communities, and the soil and waterways around vineyards are also affected. Others will suggest that it makes no sense to drink organic wine if you don't eat exclusively organic food or if you smoke cigarettes, for example. Well, humans are contradictory creatures. Nobody is saying that drinking natural wine automatically makes you an entirely ethical human being. It's one consumerist choice among many that we make each day. Ideally, natural wine prompts us to think more critically about other aspects of farming and consumption.

If you ever have a chance to visit a region like Champagne, where, because of complex inheritance laws, different vineyard growers own small parcels side-by-side, you'll see first-hand the difference between organic and conventional farming. An organic vineyard will be full of life, with wildflowers and grasses flattering vines, with rich soil composition, while a conventional plot will be bare, sometimes even with dry and cracked earth.

---

[*] In the NIH study, people who used either of the pesticides rotenone or paraquat developed Parkinson's disease at a rate 2.5 times greater than non-users.

## REGENERATIVE AGRICULTURE

The global regenerative agriculture movement has brought together growers of vines, veggies, and more who don't see themselves as organic or biodynamic. The concept here is one of restoring soil health. This might be by growing cover crops in between rows of vines, which adds nutrients back into soil, by seeding sweet peas, lupins, or even radishes. Regenerative growers could employ plant-based sprays such as nettle or calendula to help vines stay calm, cool, and resilient—the same way you'd drink a "detox" or "balance" tea to help you through a stressful period. Regenerative work might also include ecosystem or landscaping projects, such as to improve waterways, or it could be focused on carbon sequestration. A regenerative project may even use chemical sprays, but the goal is to lessen reliance on them.

## BIODYNAMIC VITICULTURE

A fascinating practice that could be summarized as farming in harmony with nature, biodynamics developed out of the concept of anthroposophy, a movement founded by philosopher Rudolf Steiner in the 1920s. Biodynamics is now a global agricultural movement, with certification through Demeter.

Biodynamic growers observe the lunar calendar, "dynamize" plant-based tinctures to spray on their vines, and encourage the biodiversity of insects and plants to ensure that vineyards are not simply chemical-free but actually thriving and more disease-resistant. A series of practices, each timed with a specific

phase of the moon, is used to create nutrient-rich, energetically imbued compost and sprays, which are then dynamized into a liquid through careful stirring in rainwater for one hour, before being applied topically to plants. The most talked-about practices of biodynamics are so-called preparations 500 and 501.*

These refer to collecting cow manure and stuffing it into cow horns (as shown on p. 75), which are then buried for six months (500); and crushing up silica (501)—both are then sprayed onto foliage. Compost is enhanced with yarrow, chamomile, and other plants that are prepared in special ways to be used as a natural fertilizer. Growers swear that practicing biodynamics over time has caused their vines to grow lovely, abundant delicious grapes.

## NON-INDUSTRIAL FARMING & NATURAL WINEMAKING

Organic, biodynamic, and regenerative practices are foundational to natural wine for a reason: Organic viticulture is known to produce healthier grapes, which means winemakers don't need to use additives to correct their harvest. Because of this, there is a necessary connection between organics and natural winemaking.

Not every producer who eschews non-industrial farming has a certification, especially if they lease vineyards rather than owning them all. They also may be "in conversion." In the absence of certification, we as consumers can seek to inform ourselves by researching a producer online or inquiring with its distributor.

Natural winemakers farm organically, biodynamically, or regeneratively not solely out of respect for the planet and concern about climate change; they do it because it improves the health of the vineyard and therefore allows them to make energetic, living wines.

---

```
*     All biodynamic preparations
are catalogued 500 to 508; there
are different theories on the
reasons, with one referring to
the fact that the Nazi regime
outlawed biodynamics, and these
numbers could have been used as
codes for surreptitious continuation.
Or they could have been created for
commercial purposes.
```

# Flower

## MARIA THUN'S BIODYNAMIC LUNAR CALENDAR

In the 1950s, a German gardener named Maria Thun expanded on Rudolf Steiner's farming lectures by experimenting with how radishes grew on different days, noting the results alongside the moon's positioning vis-à-vis the zodiac constellations.

Thun's work led to the development of the biodynamic calendar, which divides up each day of the year into four categories—"flower" and "fruit" days, which hold similar effects; and a second coupling, "root" and "leaf" days. The biodynamic calendar—used by viticulturists, agriculturists, and even dairy or livestock farmers worldwide—guides farmers through these four kinds of days along with the phases of the moon, including specific work prescriptions based on these celestial positionings.

# Root

# Fruit

Biodynamic wine-growers apply this calendar to jobs such as administering plant sprays, green-pruning or trimming, harvesting, plowing, and more. In the cellar, many producers like to apply the biodynamic calendar to important jobs such as pressing, racking, and bottling. While lunar-based agriculture would have been practiced in many societies throughout history, Thun is credited with creating a modern, practical guide.

While the biodynamic calendar may seem esoteric, it's interesting to consider the moon's gravitational pull on liquids—empirically observable in the ocean's tides.

Also intriguing is the concept that the biodynamic calendar affects how wine actually tastes—for example, a finished natural wine could taste subpar on a "root" or "leaf" day but shine brightly on a "fruit" or "flower" day. For this reason, some wine enthusiasts like to check the biodynamic calendar before opening a special bottle.

# Leaf

# NATURAL VINIFICATION: FROM JUICE TO THE BOTTLE, FEATURING WILD YEASTS

It's a tale as old as time—the love story between yeasts and sugar, a savage romance in which yeasts consume sugar to produce two main by-products: alcohol (the one we focus on) and carbon dioxide (for more on this, see Bubbles, Naturally, p. 107). It sounds like a normal, natural process—and it is. But in modern times, winemakers began subscribing to a textbook method that involved controlling fermentation through additions.

Let's walk through the whole process and establish where natural wine diverges from conventional winemaking. For small-scale, artisanal winemakers, the below is not a recipe; it's more of a spontaneous, intuition-driven "choose your own adventure" that depends on how the grapes look and taste once harvested. Remember: Wine is a spectrum, and many producers will fall somewhere in the middle, between the natural and conventional approaches outlined below.

## HARVESTING

Harvesting is the all-important step of getting the grapes off the vine, and there are myriad ways in which it can be done, each with varying effects on the quality of the grapes and the speed of the process. Generally, harvest takes place after a 90-day growing season that stretches from late spring to the advent of autumn, during which growers stay busy protecting vines from disease and supporting their growth through green-pruning and canopy management. Wineries may employ a team of seasonal or permanent workers for harvest, or it may be a family or community affair.

**NATURAL APPROACH:** Grapes are handpicked and brought directly to the winery. Often, natural winemakers favor harvesting early, aiming for more acid-driven wines while also ensuring that the grapes come in before they get too ripe and thirsty birds force their beaks through protective nets, damaging berries.

**CONVENTIONAL APPROACH:** Grapes may be handpicked or machine-harvested. In some very large-scale wineries, harvest happens elsewhere, and bulk juice is simply delivered by custom-crush facilities, removing any trace of the origins.

## SORTING

Quality isn't always consistent in the vines, whether due to animal intervention (birds pecking the grapes, wildlife snacking), differences in elevation, or weather. Sorting is the important step of examining the harvested grapes and deciding what to toss out or delegate to a lesser blend, and what to keep for a premium wine. Eyes are open for moldy, damaged, unripe, or desiccated grapes or bunches, as well as stray vine leaves.

**NATURAL APPROACH:** Winemakers pick through their harvested grapes to remove any subpar bunches, sometimes in the vineyard or more often using a sorting table. Sorting is an important step in preventing problems during fermentation. Grapes that have suffered "bird peck" are especially concerning, because they are known to develop flaws like volatile acidity (see p. 136).

**CONVENTIONAL APPROACH:** Artisanal and boutique wineries typically sort the grapes, even if they aren't striving to make natural wine. For wineries that don't prioritize quality, in lieu of sorting, the grapes are hit with a sulfur addition to deal with any bacteria, mold, or other problems.

## STEMS, SKINS, & ORANGE WINE

A grape bunch consists of the following parts:
* Stems (these connect individual grapes to each other, as well as connecting a bunch to the vine);
* Seeds (the pits within the grape);
* Skins (the outer layers of the grape);
* Juice (the liquid within the grape).

Grapes can ferment or macerate on skins if the winemaker wants the color, tannin, and flavor from those skins. Or they can be pressed right away off the skins, into juice. Ultimately, it's juice that winemakers really need. The question for producers is, at what point? In other words, all wine is pressed, but when it is pressed varies greatly.

Each winery has its own philosophy regarding skins and stems and how they are dealt with in the fermentation process. One of the most exciting points of winemaking, this sets personal styles and even regional styles apart from each other. Often, winemakers will chew on a bunch of grapes to decide whether to include the stems in fermentation, or it may depend on the variety itself and its ripening time. If stems are too "green"— that is, not ripe enough—winemakers may opt not to include them.

Once grapes are harvested, the winemaker has to make a series of choices:
* Whether to ferment the grapes "whole-bunch" (or "whole-cluster") or to destem the grapes and discard the stems;
* If destemming, what to use—either an old-fashioned wooden device where the grapes are rolled by hand, or—far more common—a modern machine;
* Stems or not, if the winemaker wants to macerate, the question remains of when to press the grapes to procure their juice.

Pressing the grapes is something that we often take for granted when we are drinking, say, a typical white wine. But the Pinot Grigio you enjoy with fish for dinner is white not by fact but because the winery chose to press the juice off the skins immediately. Had the grapes been allowed to macerate (soak), the skin contact (that is, when the juice is in contact with skins) would have resulted in slightly orange- or pink-hued juice—because Pinot Grigio has pink skins—and a more tannic, strongly flavored wine.

Red wine is always made using maceration—because otherwise the result would be a white wine made from red grapes, which is something of a waste, given the flavor that could be achieved. In other words, red wine is always a skin-contact product; the question here is simply, how long? Do winemakers leave red grapes on their skins for two weeks? One month? It depends on how extracted they want the wine to be.

**NATURAL APPROACH:** Skin contact in the natural wine world is an immensely playful, exciting topic. With the influence that the Republic of Georgia has had on global wine culture, entire regions like Italy's Friuli, on the border with Slovenia, have turned to the skin-contact winemaking that their ancestors likely would have practiced before modernizing. You can now find skin-contact whites made anywhere in the world—Oregon, East Sussex, the Languedoc…

Not all orange or skin-contact wines are necessarily natural. In fact, sometimes they are made using the technique to masquerade as natural wine. However, skin-contact white winemaking is popular among natural winemakers. Some profess that the maceration adds structure to a wine in a way that supports it during fermentation and aging, facilitating the omission of sulfites.

**CONVENTIONAL APPROACH:** Conventional winemakers, like their natural counterparts, are free to do whatever they like with skins and stems, but there is generally less creativity. In some regions, such as Burgundy, whole-cluster fermentation is quite common, whereas most commercial wineries discard the stems before fermentation. Some Burgundian wineries are known for a "lasagna" approach, where whole-bunch clusters of grapes are layered with destemmed grapes. The goal is to reduce the potential problems that whole-bunch fermentation can lead to (volatile acidity (see p. 136) being the main one), while preserving the crunchy characteristics that stems can lend.

In general, whole-cluster fermentation is seen as risky because it introduces oxygen into the wine, so most wineries tend to destem, especially those working conventionally.

## CRUSHING

Crushing grapes has several purposes, the main ones being to jump-start fermentation, to create liquid to support fermentation, and to fit a large quantity of grapes into a press.

**NATURAL APPROACH:** Some winemakers crush grapes with a machine that may be attached to the destemmer. Many natural and artisanal winemakers crush grapes as it was done for thousands of years: with a strong pair of feet.

**CONVENTIONAL APPROACH:** Machine-crushing is commonly an opportunity to add sulfites in conventional winemaking.

## FERMENTATION, PUNCH-DOWNS, & PUMP-OVERS

Now comes the most crucial stage of winemaking, especially if grapes are macerating on their skins.

As yeasts begin consuming sugar, winemakers constantly check and maintain the vat of fermenting grapes. Grapes, whether whole-bunch or destemmed, must be submerged in their own juice in order to ferment safely. Winemakers can create liquid for fermentation by foot-stomping or crushing, but as carbon dioxide forms, it's important to prevent the drying-out of the cap—a film of grapes that forms on top. To this end, winemakers perform a daily punch-down; this involves manually pressing the cap into the liquid. If the cap becomes dry, the wine gets volatile very quickly, or develops ethyl acetate. Punch-downs can be done with hands or by using a plunger-type tool.

Pump-overs, meanwhile, involve cycling the juice within the vat through the grapes to ensure that the color, tannin, and flavor are evenly distributed throughout. This is often done with a machine, though one could simply use buckets if the vessel has a tap.

If a wine has been direct-pressed to make white wine, then the fermentation process is less intensive.

**NATURAL APPROACH:** Wild yeasts are present on healthy, organic grapes, as well as in the winery environment, and they will generally start the fermentation process without too much human intervention. However, some natural winemakers add what's known as a *pied de cuve*—essentially a mash of grapes that have already fermented in a small batch—to help fermentations along and to feel secure about the yeasts that are present. Others will simply practice intense observation, checking the fermentations through smell and taste to confirm that things are going well.

**CONVENTIONAL APPROACH:** This is where commercial yeasts and yeast nutrients are added to jump-start fermentation, often with a specific formulation that's meant to result in a very particular, market-oriented taste. The goal is consistency year after year. In some regions around the world during the 20th century, it became popular to add cane sugar to wines along with artificial yeasts, a practice known as chaptalization, with the end result being a higher alcohol content; this is mostly prohibited now. Conventional wineries also practice punch-downs and pump-overs, usually with automated machines.

## CARBONIC MACERATION

In natural winemaking circles, you'll often hear people comment that a wine is "probably carbo." They might be referring to a fruity, low-acid style of wine. What they're inferring here is the use of a certain approach to fermentation that has become popular among natural winemakers for various reasons. One of those reasons is that it is a relatively safe, easy method when compared to more "traditional" fermentations.

In carbonic maceration, whole grape bunches—generally red—are put into a vat (a stainless steel or fiberglass tank, for example), and the vat is sealed. Often the winemaker will shoot some carbon dioxide into the vat before closing it, but even without this step, carbon dioxide will slowly fill the vat and prevent the presence of any oxygen as the grapes begin to ferment. At a certain moment, the winemaker will open the vat and press the grapes.

The carbonic maceration technique was invented by accident in 1934, when a French research team experimented with storing fresh grapes with carbon dioxide for several months, and the surprise result was a pleasant flavor. Certain regions, like Beaujolais, have become a hotbed of carbonic maceration—the technique seems to suit Gamay well. It's a likable approach in part because the anaerobic environment—the absence of oxygen—ensures grapes can ferment safely, with zero maintenance required during the time they are in the vat. There is a reduced risk of problems because the grapes aren't exposed to air as they are in traditional fermentation styles; there's also less work required, because there is no need to perform daily punch-downs and pump-overs. For a producer with limited help in the winery in a busy harvest season, a carbonic maceration would be a great way to initiate fermentation.

The result for the drinker is generally a fruity, easygoing, aromatic wine that is less tannic and acidic than a traditionally fermented one. However, there are complaints that "all carbo wines taste the same," due to carbonic maceration producing flavors that mask the varietal characteristics of the grape itself or the terroir. You might consider carbo wines along the same lines of the *glou glou* style: wines to be enjoyed with friends at a picnic or as a starter to a meal.

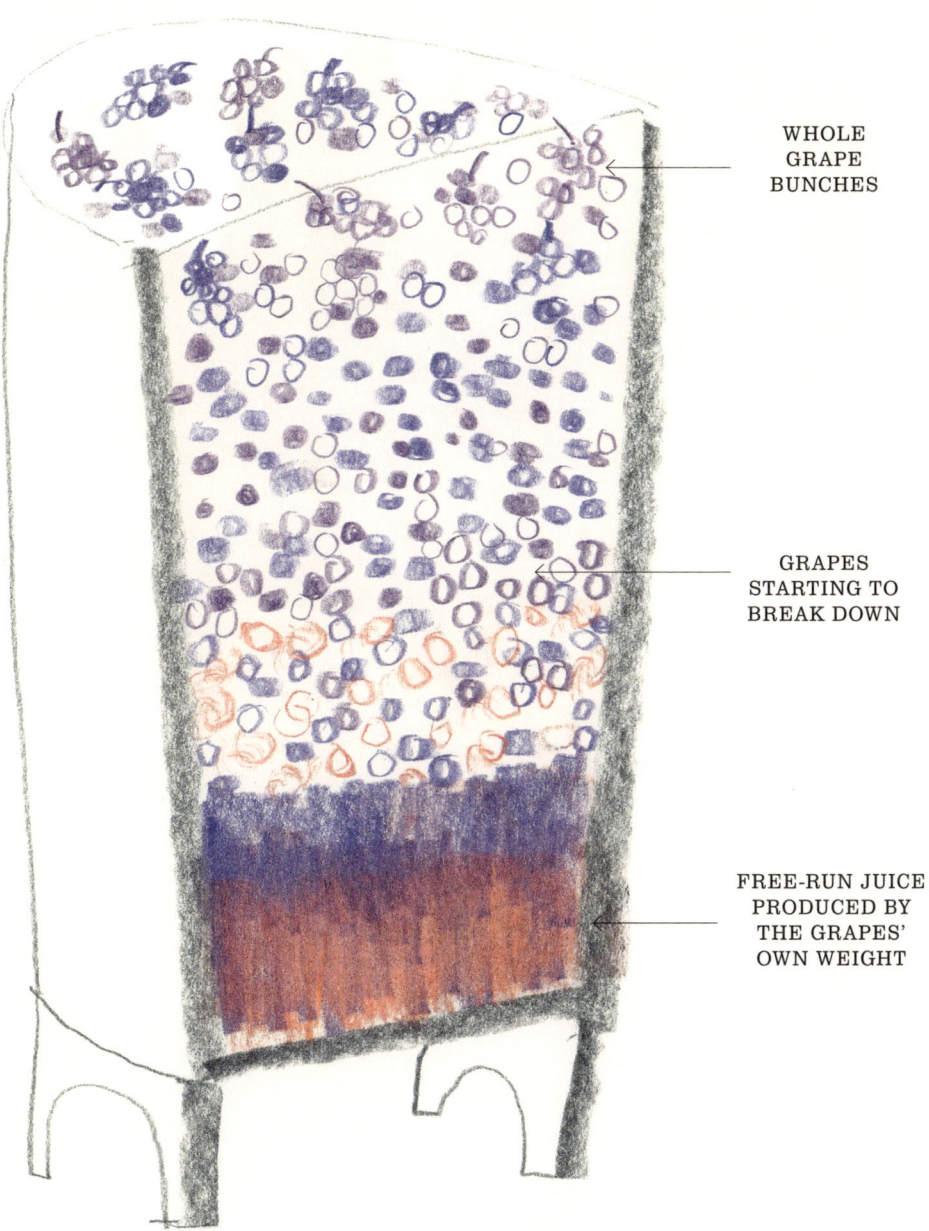

## PRIMARY & MALOLACTIC FERMENTATIONS

Left to its own devices, wine goes through two stages of **fermentation: primary**, then **malolactic**.

An important consideration for both fermentations is what vessel they occur in. Winemakers decide this based on the variety and style they are working with; common choices include wooden barrels or vats, stainless-steel tanks, fiberglass tanks, concrete tanks, ceramic amphorae or "eggs," glass demijohns, or really anything else that suits the quantity and desired quality.

The vat makes a big difference: It allows the wine to come into contact with differing amounts of oxygen; affects how malolactic fermentation occurs; and may impart some flavor, especially if wood is used. For natural winemakers, choosing a vessel that reduces heat, such as ceramic, is an excellent way to control temperature.

**NATURAL APPROACH:** Natural winemakers allow primary fermentation to happen with wild indigenous yeasts. They also allow the full malolactic process to occur, resulting in a rounder-bodied wine.

Primary fermentation: A yeast-driven process whereby sugar is converted into alcohol and carbon dioxide.

Malolactic fermentation: A bacteria-driven process that converts tart malic acid into softer lactic acid. It is often abbreviated to malo or MLF.

**CONVENTIONAL APPROACH:** Often, commercial yeasts are added; these may be neutral or flavored—to help the wine taste the way consumers expect it to. Many conventional wineries add sulfites to arrest fermentation before the malolactic conversion takes place; conversely, they may even induce malolactic through inoculation of certain bacterial strains.

A main focus of conventional wineries during fermentation is artificial temperature control. Stainless-steel tanks can be fitted with cooling jackets, through which coolant runs, slowing things down; or the winery will be air-conditioned—the goal being to make sure fermentation happens at a certain pace. In very large wineries, the latter is often managed by a central computer system.

This is also the point at which wineries may use numerous additives intended to alter the flavor and body of a wine, including but not limited to colorants, acidulants, and tannins/wood chips.

# PRESSING

At some point before, during, or after fermentation, the winemaker decides to press the juice out of the grapes (known as pressing off the skins). This may be an earlier step if they want a non-macerated (such as a white or direct-press) wine, or it may be done after several days or several weeks. Whatever the timing, the fermentation vat must be emptied and its contents loaded into a press. Most winemakers these days use pneumatic (electric) presses in which an air-filled bag rolls over the grapes until all the juice has been pushed out into a tray below; others still use traditional, manually operated (sometimes hydraulic), vertically oriented basket presses, where the juice flows out into a bucket or vat.

**NATURAL APPROACH:** The main consideration for pressing wine without additions is protecting the juice. Natural winemakers who follow the biodynamic calendar may choose to press on "fruit" days, to highlight the fruit flavors.

**CONVENTIONAL APPROACH:** Much the same as for natural wines, but the pressed juice generally receives a sulfite addition.

## FILTRATION, RACKING, & LEES AGING

There's stuff in your natural wine that makes it cloudy. In French, the term for this is *vin trouble*. Yes, our wine is troubled. Actually, it's fine—it's just unfiltered.

An unfiltered wine may have some sediment consisting of an accumulation of tartrates and lees. Tartrates form when the naturally occurring tartaric acid in grapes binds with potassium and calcium under cold conditions. Lees are a different, more useful by-product of winemaking that play a role in its flavor. When you ferment grapes and the yeasts consume sugar, eventually some of those yeasts die and they accumulate. If there is skin contact at all, these dead yeasts will mingle with the leftover grape skins. This mixture is known as the lees. When you press fermenting grapes, the juice will contain lees. As time passes, the juice rises and the lees sink. The lees continue to influence the wine, adding texture and flavor.

Some producers like to stir the lees by submerging a large whisk into a barrel. This practice is known as *bâttonage*, and it is one way of giving that classic buttery note to Chardonnay. Ultimately, however, the lees should not end up in the bottle.

When it's time to bottle wine, you ideally lift the finished wine off its lees through a process called **racking**.

Filtration and fining are related techniques. Filtration can focus on larger particles, or it can sterilize the wine through a microscopic membrane; the process aims to remove particles, stabilize the wine, and, in its more extreme version, present crystal-clear rosé or pale-yellow white wine to consumers. Fining, on the other hand, uses a substance (sometimes egg whites) to bind together all the material in a wine, then remove it. For more on fining, see Is Natural Wine Vegan? on p. 66.

Will you encounter a bee or a whole grape floating around in a bottle of natural wine at some point? Possibly. And when you do, consider it a rite of passage. You're drinking something so closely connected to the place it's from, you even got a little critter in your glass. Think of the unfiltered matter in your glass as the stuff of life—the life of the vineyard, the life of the winery, the life all around you as you consume this wine.

**Racking:** Transferring juice/wine from one vat to another, typically by funneling through a hose. Often gas is used to propel the liquid; or in a well-designed winery, gravity can be employed. The goal is sometimes to remove the juice/wine from the lees that have accumulated at the bottom of the vat.

**NATURAL APPROACH:** Many natural and artisanal producers do not filter their wines—you'll generally be able to tell because there will be a little sediment in the bottle. Some might do the minimum of passing the wine through a sieve before bottling. Other self-described natural winemakers prefer a gentle filtration. They may use a cartridge that collects particles before bottling or instead employ a centrifugal machine that spins the wine to separate and remove the solids.

Winemakers who follow the lunar calendar generally prefer to rack wine during a waning moon, to encourage stability.

**CONVENTIONAL APPROACH:** It is common for conventional wineries to filter and fine using advanced technologies, with the goal being minimal turbidity (by reducing the presence of solids) and delivering the crystal-clear look of many supermarket wines.

## SETTLING & AGING

After racking, there is usually a short period of settling to allow any captured lees to sink to the bottom. Then the important process of aging, when a wine's flavors integrate and its structure improves.

Every wine has a different aging regime. Some will age in the same vessel they've fermented in, while others need to be racked into a new vessel, where they will stay until it's time for bottling. During this period, the wine will evaporate, particularly if it's aging in wood vessels, and winemakers will top up the levels using wine they've set aside for this purpose, so as to prevent oxidation (a chemical reaction resulting from exposure to oxygen; see p. 137).

**NATURAL APPROACH:** This isn't exclusive to naturalists, but there's a growing preference for aging in ceramic vessels, which is not only the ancient way of aging wine but is also known to provide a cooling neutral, breathable environment in which the wine can develop. Some winemakers, for stylistic reasons, do not top up their wines, favoring the development of a "veil" on top of their wine that deliberately creates an oxidative flavor; this approach is traditional in the Jura region of France.

**CONVENTIONAL APPROACH:** Aging is another chance to add sulfites, and in very conventional wineries it's also the point at which a wine's flavor and appearance are adjusted through numerous additives, including colorants, acidulants, artificial tannins, and so on. Alternatively, these may have been added during fermentation.

# CLEANING

There's a saying that 50 percent of winemaking is cleaning. And it's hardly a joke: Without good hygiene procedures, a winery can become a harbor for bacteria and therefore an unsafe workplace. Virtually all wineries use quite a bit of water, hosing down the press after use and even the floors and walls—often with a pressure washer. But as with all things wine, there's a spectrum from natural to commercial that applies to cleaning practices.

**NATURAL APPROACH:** In the depths of European wine country, moldy bottles dating back a century are proudly displayed in underground cellars dug into hillsides. These pre-modern wine caves were originally created for natural temperature control, not for sanitation—and you will rarely see a freshly scrubbed surface here. Instead, the presence of mold is seen as normal, and the place is left alone. Meanwhile, other natural winemakers have impeccably clean, modern fermentation rooms—but they mostly use hot water and light soaps, rather than harsh detergents.

Sulfur dioxide may be used as a cleaning agent in barrels, which, if left empty, are at risk of developing unhealthy bacteria, yeasts, and molds. Sometimes you'll see a wire sticking out of the barrel hole—that's a sulfur candle that has been lowered into the vessel and burned.

Many natural winemakers stress that cleaning is even more important in their cellars than in conventional ones, because natural wine doesn't rely on correctives. But the goal isn't to eliminate microbial life completely; it's important to protect the native yeast population to ensure that fermentation can occur on its own.

**CONVENTIONAL APPROACH:** When wine is mass-produced, the environment is sterilized as much as possible. No romantic old caves here—just regular and constant disinfecting, cleaning, and sanitizing with food-grade commercial detergents. Barrels are rigorously washed with sulfur dioxide.

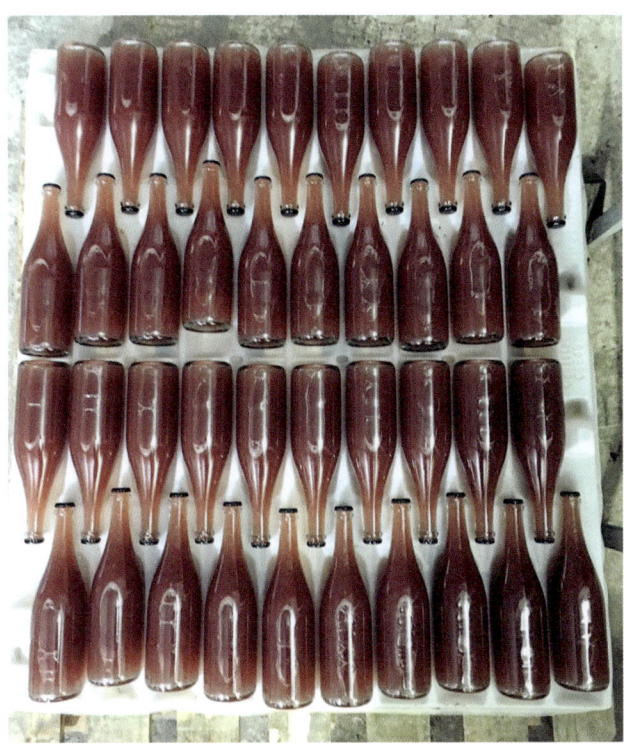

## BOTTLING

The decision of when to bottle a wine depends on numerous factors, the most important being whether it has fully achieved its flavor potential and has fermented completely dry. A wine can also age in bottle, where its flavors coalesce and tannins integrate to become part of the overall profile.

**NATURAL APPROACH:** Bottling is the point at which natural winemakers tend to add *minimal* sulfites, the goal being to prevent the wine from refermenting in bottle. What's "minimal" is entirely subjective, but it may be anything between 5 and 20ppm. Other winemakers add nothing and simply hope for the best, knowing that this "living" wine will continue transforming.

**CONVENTIONAL APPROACH:** By the time of bottling, wines may already have 50–70ppm of added sulfites and will likely receive an additional dose.

# STAGES OF NATURAL VINIFICATION

Every wine follows its own unique trajectory, which may include some or all of the steps below, or variations on them. Winemakers decide based on the vintage, the quality of the fruit, and the desired style, how to proceed.

1 — HARVESTING ⟶ 2 — SORTING ⟶

CARBONIC MACERATION

→ 3 — STEMS, SKINS, & ORANGE WINE → 4 — CRUSHING

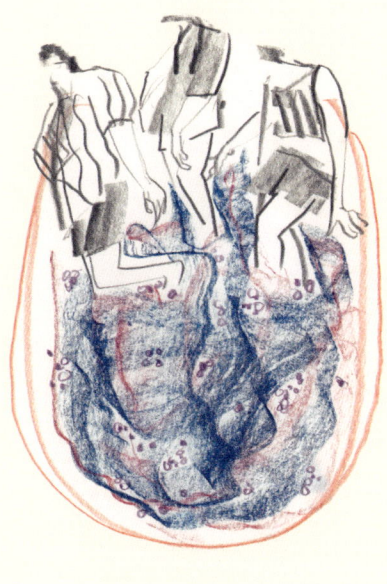

*continues overleaf*    97

5 — FERMENTATION, PUNCH-DOWNS, & PUMP-OVERS → 6 — PRESSING

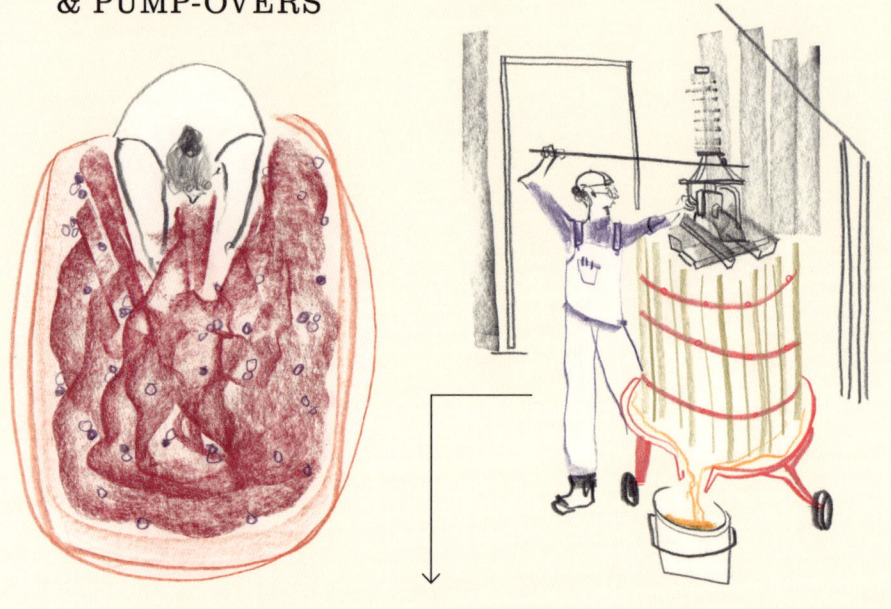

7 — CLEANING

# 9 – SETTLING & AGING

→ 10 – BOTTLING

→ 8 – RACKING

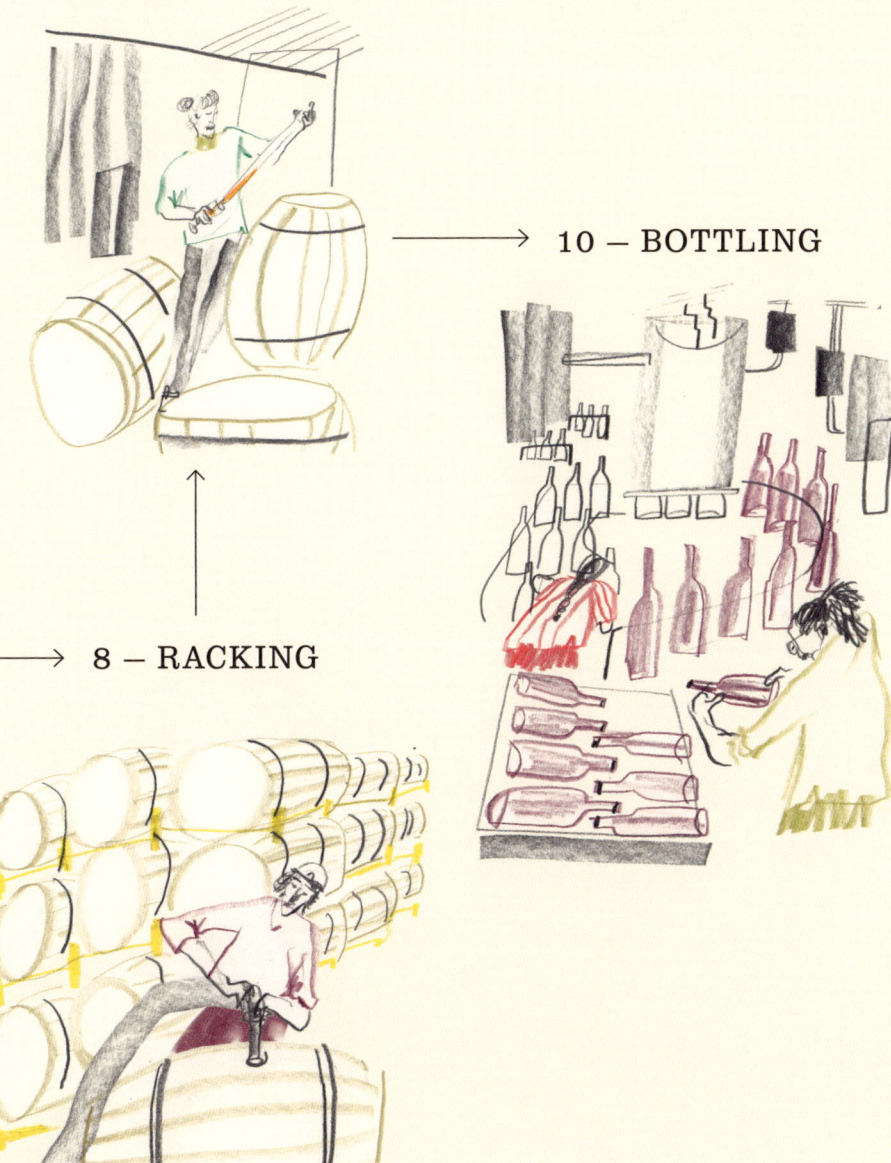

# THE ART OF FERMENTATION: A PERSONAL ANECDOTE

In my second year of winemaking, we harvested some Chardonnay grapes on quite a hot day. That evening, I pressed the grapes and poured the juice straight from the press into a barrel. Within days, the fermentation was going strong—perhaps too strong. Foam was pouring out of the barrel nonstop, and I could hardly manage to keep a bubble airlock in the bunghole. This simple device, which allows carbonation to flow out so the barrel can be partially closed without exploding, just wouldn't stay on.

The result was a wine that was very high in volatile acidity (see p. 136). Thanks to its unruly fermentation, it was basically undrinkable: aggressively alcoholic, with notes of nail-polish remover that masked the fruit itself.

Years later, I'm still using the last bottles from that batch to braise osso buco in winter. I could have managed the fermentation through sulfites, temperature control, and commercial yeasts, and the whole situation would have been avoided. But that's not the kind of wine I wanted to make, and I learned from my mistakes. Since that fateful vintage, I have only fermented Chardonnay in cooling ceramic vessels, and I haven't had a problem since.

# YOU SAY GRAPES, WE SAY BIODIVERSITY: A NATURALIST UNDERSTANDING OF VINE-GROWING

**What happens in the cellar is only half the battle. Wine is made first in the vineyard, and the work there goes on year-round: winter pruning and spring pruning, sowing cover crops, and dealing with grass and weeds are just a few of the main jobs.**

But before all that, there is the question of planting vines—a massive job that involves deep knowledge and important decisions. Many natural and artisanal winemakers are invested in growing vines with respect for biodiversity and concern for climate change. This could mean cultivating rare heirloom varieties, or focusing on massal selection as the principal method of cloning, or embracing polycultural farming versus monoculture.

## HEIRLOOM GRAPE VARIETIES

Enough of Cabernet, Chardonnay, and Merlot in regions they don't originate from, natural winemakers say—instead, they are cultivating unique varieties that are considered indigenous to their region. By preserving indigenous grape varieties, these winemakers ensure that we can not only enjoy different kinds of wines (imagine drinking the same three grapes over and over; variety is what makes wine exciting) but also that the world's vineyards have a future. An indigenous or heirloom variety has acclimatized itself to a region for centuries and has been selected over time for its resilience, unlike international clones. We should be grateful that today we can drink wine made of Romorantin, a vibrant white grape with a lemony character, and Pineau d'Aunis, a heavenly red grape with peppery tones. These two extremely rare grapes grow exclusively in the Loire Valley and have been kept alive thanks to the natural wine movement there.

## MASSAL SELECTION

This is the traditional farmer's way of creating new vinestock. It involves subjectively selecting individual grapevines that show desirable traits and taking **cuttings**. Massal selection is a traditional approach that preserves vineyard heritage, unlike cloning. In the latter, we take genetic material from one "mother vine" and propagate it en masse, with consistency being the goal. Commercial clones dominate the wine world, and the result is a loss of genetic diversity in grapevines. We see the same Chardonnay clone or the same Pinot Noir clone again and again. Wines start to lose their unique character, their terroir.

**Cuttings:** Pieces of a vine that are used for vegetative propagation.

**Grafting:** A horticultural technique whereby plant tissues are joined to continue growing together as a single plant.

**Rootstock:** The base of a vine that supplies a grafted vine with a root system. Grapevine rootstocks are derived from American *Vitis* species that are resistant to phylloxera. In some parts of the world where phylloxera isn't a risk, cuttings can be planted directly into the ground; these are referred to as own-rooted vines.

## GRAFTING

Most vineyards are planted through a process of **grafting**, whether massal selection or mother-vine clones have been used. Cuttings from either source are grafted onto **rootstock** that is resistant to a vicious pest called phylloxera, which once wiped out nearly all of Europe's vineyards. Consider that you can raise Sauvignon Blanc seedlings from cuttings then graft them onto any rootstock, and the vine will simply change its genetic material and grow Sauvignon Blanc— aren't vines amazing?

## POLYCULTURE

Vineyards as far as the eye can see? Sure, it's beautiful—but it's also monoculture, which can be hard on the soil and on wildlife. Furthermore, it could allow for quicker spread of pests or diseases. Farmers around the world practice polyculture, and many have been doing this for centuries: fruit orchards, grapevines, grain, honey, and animals together in the same place, encouraging a flourishing, harmonious organic ecosystem.

## BIODIVERSITY FOR THE FUTURE OF WINE

If all of the above sounds a little daunting, you're not alone—viticulturists study and apprentice in the arts of propagation, planting, and pruning for years.

Perhaps it helps to think about the spectrum of grape variety quality through the lens of tomatoes. If you've experienced the sensation of biting into the flesh of a ripe heirloom tomato, compare that to a supermarket tomato. It's not just that one is organic; the varieties make a difference. Modern grapevine clones, like modern tomatoes, can be lacking in character and flavor.

Many natural winemakers are lucky to have tiny vineyard plots so old that they simply never stopped farming the old way, through organics and massal selection, while others are consciously moving in this direction. In the face of climate change, it seems that one of the keys to the future of the wine industry will be preserving biodiversity. Supporting natural wine is intrinsic to this effort because it keeps indigenous varieties alive.

# BUBBLES, NATURALLY

It never ceases to amaze me that wine, already a perfect thing, can be made so much more enjoyable through the presence of bubbles—and how incredible that it's possible to have gorgeous bubbles while adding absolutely nothing: no sugar, no gas. Just the magic of nature.

In fermentation, one of the by-products of yeasts consuming sugar is carbon dioxide. To make a naturally sparkling wine, one approach is to monitor the wine during fermentation, watching as sugar levels go down while alcohol rises—then, at just the right moment, while there is still some sugar left, bottle the wine. In the bottle, the wine continues fermenting, and the leftover carbon dioxide is trapped in there, causing bubbles. This is known as the ancestral method, and the resultant wine style as *pétillant-naturel*, or pét-nat.

Alternatively, a producer may freeze freshly crushed grapes (known as must), then add that to dry wine just before bottling, to restart fermentation in the bottle.

These methods stand in contrast to the famed traditional method, in which a wine ferments dry, then is bottled with an addition of yeast and sugar. Champagne, Crémant, and Franciacorta are all made by the traditional method.

Prosecco wines, meanwhile, are generally made with the Charmat method, in which a tank of dry, finished wine is put into a pressurized tank and dosed with yeast and sugar. The Charmat method results in an approachable wine that's suitable for mixing with orange juice for mimosas.

Naturally sparkling wine is unique because it's made without any additives. Sometimes, though, in a naturally sparkling wine there is *too much* carbon dioxide—resulting in a

# it's very special to enjoy a sparkling wine made with grapes only

bottle that bursts open, wine spewing everywhere. There will also be a lot of sediment in the wine: dead yeasts and tartrates, residues of fermentation.

Enter disgorgement (see p. 30). You've most likely heard of disgorging in relation to Champagne, but naturally sparkling wines benefit from it, too. Bottled wines are stored upside down to allow the sediment to accumulate in the necks, and the necks are frozen to help solidify the sediment. Next, the bottles are popped open one by one, and the frozen sediment flies out (along with some wine). At this point, they are refilled (usually with the same wine) and recapped—or sometimes sealed with a Champagne cork. Ideally, the wines then rest for a few months before going to market.

Making pét-nat this way is very labor-intensive, not to mention the time needed for the extra aging. But it's very special to enjoy a sparkling wine made with grapes only. No added yeasts or sugars, and ideally no sulfites, are necessary to achieve a beautiful, artisanal sparkling wine.

Perhaps the most endearing aspect of pét-nat is that there are no restrictions on what grapes may be used. You can find single-variety pét-nats, blended pét-nats, rosé pét-nats, and skin-contact white (orange) pét-nats. The pét-nat world is your oyster—and yes, that's a truly perfect pairing.

# EXPERT VIEW: WHAT'S THE BIG DEAL WITH SULFITES?

## WITH AUSTRALIAN SCIENTIST & NATURAL WINEMAKER ALEX SCHULKIN

Sulfur dioxide, also known as $SO_2$, is a gas that's generally manufactured but also occurs in nature (particularly when a volcano erupts). As the compound name implies, it is a sulfur atom with two oxygen atoms attached. When added to liquid, $SO_2$ becomes ions known as sulfites.

The practice of adding sulfites to wine during its fermentation journey is something that generates much controversy within the natural wine industry. Some producers add "minimal amounts" (a subjective term that could mean between 5 and 20ppm), while others add zero.

The addition of sulfites doesn't indicate something ethical or moral about the producer, but within the industry, people stake out camps of "adding sulfites" or "not adding sulfites" as if they were taking sides in a war. For many, it's a question of personal taste, while for others it's a commercial matter, since no-sulfite wine can be more delicate to handle, sell, and serve.

Adding sulfites stabilizes a wine by killing bacteria. It also arrests the development of the wine to an extent—meaning it limits its changeability. Unsulfured wines can also achieve stability, depending on how they are made.

Most wines do contain naturally occurring sulfites regardless of whether the producer added anything. They may have been generated during fermentation or potentially were present in the soil. You'll see the phrase "contains sulfites" on most wine labels as a result, but it can be misleading—for example, in the US, a wine may have zero detectable naturally occurring sulfites, but unless samples are sent to an administrative body ahead of shipment, the producer must include "contains sulfites" on the label. Few have the time or money for such bureaucratic hurdles.

Australian natural winemaker Alex Schulkin is also a researcher at the prestigious Australian Wine Research Institute. With expertise in enology and wine chemistry, Schulkin

# the wine is not yours to control

can address what sulfites actually do in winemaking. Under the label The Other Right, he produces wines that are juicy, light, and full of personality. Since 2016, he has worked without adding sulfites. Here Schulkin shares some of his knowledge and experience.

**WHAT DOES ADDING SULFITES DO TO A WINE?**
The amount of sulfites isn't as important as *when* they're added. What I personally appreciate so much about wild fermentation is its complexity, in how so many different organisms get a chance to play a role. When juice is hit with sulfites at the very start, fermentation can still be spontaneous—it can happen without adding yeasts—but it won't be the same. Not adding sulfites is partly about embracing the fact that the wine is not yours to control and about acknowledging its right to self-determination, philosophically speaking. We still very much make the wine, but we prefer to meddle as little as possible, especially with the wine's microflora. With added sulfites, a wine still evolves but in a much lesser manner.

## ARE SULFITES BAD FOR YOU, AND DO THEY CAUSE A HANGOVER?

A single piece of [sulfur-treated] dried fruit has much higher levels of sulfites than an entire bottle of wine. It's difficult to compare, maybe, but the point is, consuming sulfites in wine isn't bad for you. It is an allergen for around one percent of the population. In terms of hangovers, the correlation is generally with alcohol, not sulfites.

## SO, WHY SHOULD CONSUMERS CARE IF SULFITES ARE ADDED?

It's about the winemaker's reason for not using sulfites. When you look at a wine, you have to consider the winemaker's intention the way you think about a work of art. Some artists choose charcoal, while others paint with oil. Nobody questions why one artist uses paint and the other uses charcoal—because it's how that artist thinks they can make the most out of the image they have and the canvas or paper they're making it on. Winemakers are the same. There are as many opinions as there are winemakers.

## WHY DO YOU PERSONALLY CHOOSE NOT TO ADD SULFITES TO YOUR WINES?

On my journey, I decided that I wanted to work with grapes only. That's the best wine I can make. To me, using only grapes is the purest form of winemaking. It takes courage not to add sulfites. You're deliberately taking the risk of spoiled wine. But art is not rational either. Three years ago, I had a crisis of genre, and I was reassessing my sulfites stance. Was it not disrespectful to growers if I made wine with their fruit and it failed, and I then had to throw it out? Then I came to terms with the fact that the proportion of success is actually very high. Some wines also have problems, and then they recover.

## DO YOU PREFER TO DRINK ONLY NO-SULFITE-ADDED WINES?

Not all wines without sulfites are great, and not all with sulfites added are terrible. When you talk about flaws, I also have to say that some wines are perfectly sound but also very boring.

# WHAT IS TERROIR?
# AND WHAT DOES NATURAL
# WINE HAVE TO DO WITH IT?

In the old, old days, it was common knowledge which town excelled at growing onions and which one produced the nicest hard grain. Similarly, as people in the Levant began to cultivate grapevines many thousands of years before the Common Era, they also noticed which kinds of grapes flourished in certain places. One of our greatest historians of wine, the ancient Roman Pliny the Elder, commits this knowledge to the page when he ranks the wines of central Italy: "Who can entertain a doubt that some kinds of wine are more agreeable to the palate than others, or that even out of the very same vat there are occasionally produced wines that are by no means of equal goodness, [...] whether it is that it is owing to the cask, or to some other fortuitous circumstance?" He then goes on to list each wine in the top ranking and specify exactly where it grows: "The wine is grown near a bay of the Adriatic [...] where the sea-breeze ripens a few grapes."*

\* From the Perseus/Tufts University translation, "Chap. 8. (6.)—Fifty Kinds of Generous Wines."

At its heart, terroir is this: an understanding of how a place shapes its wines, through elements in the climate (wind, temperature, general weather); geological factors (soil, bedrock, elevation); and, importantly, living culture (human traditions, farming practices, animal and microbial life). A wine made with respect for terroir is a wine that is allowed to reflect its place. This could mean a single bottling comes from a single parcel, but it can also be a blend made with consideration of an entire area or region.

The concept of terroir was forgotten as commercial and bulk wine production took hold, and also because industrialization drew young people away from viticultural areas, removing the lineage through which knowledge could be passed down. With the resurgence of artisanal and natural wine at the end of the 20th century, the reborn, postmodern concept of terroir finds itself in a tug-of-war between winemaking ideologies. According to one argument, any wine made with added yeasts, temperature control, and filtration is manipulated to the point where no terroir is discernible. Meanwhile, the other side argues that producing an unfiltered wine without sulfites actually loses the terroir, because all of these wines ultimately taste similar.

In my experience, terroir is an elusive thing that is difficult to pin down. Recently, I had a no-sulfite-added wine made from a vineyard on Mount Etna in Sicily. The wine was made by a Frenchman, and to me it tasted utterly French. Interesting… Problematic? Does a van Gogh landscape really look like the location where the painter stood, or does it reflect more what's in the painter's mind? Humans have egos that are difficult to hide. And terroir is an evolving concept—a question that we are constantly asking rather than a fixable thing. Even if the soils remain the same, the climate changes and the culture evolves.

As you taste more and more wine, you'll form your own opinions. If you're curious to investigate terroir, the aforementioned Mount Etna region is a very exciting place to do that, along with Burgundy (in France), where terroir is so embedded in the winemaking that each vineyard has a classification along with renowned attributes. In New World wine regions, terroir is a much newer notion, without millennia of history, so there is even more to explore.

# terroir is an elusive thing that is difficult to pin down

# CHAOS THEORY MEETS NATURAL WINE: A CONVERSATION WITH AUSTRIAN WINE-GROWERS GUT OGGAU

Only 15 years ago, most wine drinkers would frown at the mention of the Burgenland region. Despite having some of the oldest evidence of winemaking in western Europe and the presence of stunning Lake Neusiedl, the warm, flat area close to Vienna didn't have a reputation for quality artisanal winemaking. Instead, the Burgenland was producing mostly bulk wine with the red grapes Blaufränkisch and Zweigelt.

With the rise of natural wine, that all changed. Careful vineyard management and thoughtful fermentation showed the world that Burgenland terroir could produce excellent wines. Numerous producers had a hand in this, notably Pittnauer, Christian Tschida, Claus Preisinger, Judith Beck, and the Rennersistas.

Meanwhile, a particularly striking label began appearing in wine bars around the world, featuring nothing more than the name Gut Oggau—which simply references the town itself—and a sketch of a face, always a different one on each cuvée. Gut Oggau soon took the natural wine world by storm with these mysterious wines, a wide range that offered no information about which grape varieties were used. The wines—overall light and lively—conveyed a joyous quality, and each bottle somehow left you wanting more.

Today, Eduard and Stephanie Tscheppe of Gut Oggau are known not just for the intrigue of their wines but also for insisting that the focus of natural wine is the vineyard. They emphasize that "everything is connected," and that farming their vineyards with biodynamic practices is only one part of a holistic lifestyle and broader philosophy of nature. In 2025, they gave a public talk on this topic, which we continued discussing the next day. What follows is an edited and condensed version of that conversation, including some quotes from their talk.

## GUT OGGAU

There are facts we cannot deny in the world: erosion of the soil, pollution, decaying species. Modern agriculture is causing problems. According to modern agriculture, all you need to grow plants are water, nutrients, and sun. But there is an ancient approach that goes beyond the material to the energetic.

To paraphrase physicist Max Planck, "We will never understand the miracle of nature, because we are part of it." There's another saying: If a butterfly flaps its wings in China, it changes the weather in Europe. If you do something within the system, you change the system. For that reason, we are not winemakers, we are *viticulteurs*, as the French say—wine-growers.

Consider the idea of chaos theory: From order, things descend into chaos, and then they return to order. It's the way plants grow: A grain of rye emerges on the plant, it becomes seed. Then it germinates on the ground, where it falls back into chaos; it is digested into the soil to become a new order. Whatever chaos we're in, there will be order.

When you farm in the industralized way, you purchase resources from outside to grow products, which results in waste like pollution, erosion, and the death of insects and animals. The costs of the waste are borne by society. We farm in a closed-loop system, using manure from our animals as fertilizer and cover crops to regenerate the soil.

Our journey began in 2007, when we found an abandoned winery that was known for quality. When we started Gut Oggau, we joined a group where we still today make our biodynamic preps together. Every year, we take another step into biodynamics. We can always add more vitality to the soil. Now we are planting 120 trees each year, taking carbon dioxide from the atmosphere and fixing it in the ground.

When people began making wine, eight thousand years ago in the Caucasus, they made it for cultural gatherings. It was about a connection to higher beings. The vine is an amazing plant; it has such a deep connection with soil. It's been cultivated in arid regions, so it can go deep and collect information from the soil. That's why it provides a sense of place, terroir.

Wine is also incredible because it's a fermented product that you can age. It allows you to time-travel because it brings you to the time it was grown.

An energetic wine can only come from a healthy vineyard. When tasting healthy grapes from healthy vines, the taste itself isn't so important because the wine changes every day—and anyway, taste is subjective. More important is, how does the wine make you feel?

Wine is preserved energy from the vine in a glass. And that energy will do us good, because it's from the cosmos. And we need that. We're on computers all day. Maybe if you can have a glass of wine, it uplifts you.

# 3

# CHOOSING, POURING, ENJOYING

# A NO-RULES CULTURE

**The best thing about the rules of natural wine? There are none.**

This isn't the world of the **WSET** and sommeliers wearing suits and pins. Nobody cares if you know anything about appellations. Exploring natural wine is a social process, involving supporting local businesses, sharing wines with friends, and reading on your own (just as you're doing now).

An important first step is to find a reliable wine shop where the staff has experience and knowledge. Over time, you'll learn which styles, price points, producers, and regions suit the mood or occasion you are shopping for. There are several online vendors of natural wine with excellent offerings. But if you can find a bricks-and-mortar shop near you, you'll have the luxury of being able to ask questions while browsing the bottles, and to have conversations after you've enjoyed a beguiling wine that left you wondering about its farming or vinification.

You'll *need* to ask questions, because natural wine labels are notoriously vague. Sometimes this is for legal reasons; often, when winemakers are refused access to the appellation, they cannot name the place or grape variety on a wine label. Additionally, many natural winemakers like to work with blends, and rather than list every grape variety that goes into the wine, they give it a "fantasy name" and hope that you'll try it based on the color or on a hunch that it's good.

Consider purchasing wines in packs of three or six from the same region, to get to know the typical grape varieties of that area. Or focus on a few producers you like, slowly familiarizing yourself with their various cuvées.

**WSET: The Wine & Spirit Education Trust runs renowned qualification courses for wine professionals.**

# DECODING A NATURAL WINE LABEL

A natural wine label can be like a work of abstract art: visually striking, perhaps controversial, and often difficult to understand without context. Then there's the problem of what to do with a label that's written partly in a foreign language.

Think of a natural wine label as containing coded data. It helps if you know the basics of the lexicon. The following is a general guide to what you might find on a natural wine label, and what it means when you're choosing a bottle.

**PRODUCER NAME:** This may be a business or brand name, such as Domaine de l'Octavin, or it could be the winemaker's exact name, like Alice Bouvot. Sometimes, both will be present on the label.

**CUVÉE NAME:** Also known as a fantasy name, a cuvée name is what the winemaker has chosen to call a specific bottling, and it often conveys the way a winemaker sees the product. There's usually a story behind the name: Nuits d'Ivresse, a Cabernet Franc from Catherine and

Pierre Breton in the Loire Valley, means "nights of drunkenness" and references a film; Franco Terpin's Quinto Quarto means "fifth quarter," which is an Italian term for offal; La Cerretina is a Pācina white blend named for a specific oak tree planted in the vineyard—just to mention a few interesting examples.

**REGION:** Often, natural winemakers are barred from their appellation, so you may not see official geographic designations such as Rhône Valley AOC or Chianti Classico on these bottles; more likely, a generic national title such as Vin de France ("wine of France") is all that's permitted. However, there will be an address featuring the location of the winery, which you can use to research the region of the winemaker.

**APPELLATION:** An appellation is a legally protected region unified by certain traditional practices—for example, Côtes du Rhône is a popular appellation that encompasses a specific geographic area, specific grape varieties and even a minimum alcohol content (among other rules). New World regions do not tend to have strict appellations as such.

**VINTAGE:** The year written on the bottle is the vintage (harvest season) when the grapes were gathered and the wine made. Sometimes, the winemaker is prohibited from displaying the vintage, so instead you might find a clue in something called a lot number, where "23" could indicate the 2023 vintage.

**VARIETY:** Many natural winemakers either choose not to include or are prohibited from including the grape variety on their label, while others do mention it, either on the front or on the back label along with a description of the wine.

**ALCOHOL CONTENT:** By law, a wine bottle must display the percentage of its volume that contains alcohol (ABV, or alcohol by volume).

# think of a natural wine label as containing coded data

**PREGNANCY WARNING:** In some countries, wine labels must feature a symbol showing a pregnant woman with a line across the image.

**VOLUME:** It is a legal requirement to include the capacity of the bottle on the label, which in most instances will be 75cl, though one-liter bottles occasionally make an appearance, and the rare 50cl bottle can be found.

**CERTIFICATION:** Some wines display a farming certification on their labels, from bodies such as Ecocert in France, both indicating certified organic winegrowing. Internationally, the Demeter stamp is used on certified biodynamic wines.

**"CONTAINS SULFITES":** As previously mentioned (see p. 111), this legally required statement is more or less meaningless when it comes to natural wines. Some producers choose to write "only naturally occurring sulfites" or "without added sulfites."

**IMPORTER:** Usually on the back label, the importer's name can become an important signifier for you as a purchaser of natural wines. Over time, observe which importer labels keep showing up when you enjoy a wine, and you'll come to have a sense of their portfolio, which then becomes a shopping hack when you're exploring a new store or unknown producers.

# WE'VE GOT THE FUNK: TASTING & DESCRIBING NATURAL WINES

If you watch a documentary on conventional wine culture—such as 2013's **Somm**, which follows a handful of professionals preparing for the rigorous Master Sommelier exam—you'll be struck by the very particular words used to describe wine flavors: "Star bright. Medium concentration. Moderate-plus intensity. Very young. Chalky limestone minerality."*

In a natural wine crowd, it would be unusual to hear such analytic descriptions of a wine. It's not that natural wine drinkers don't have refined palates; it's that we're less focused on categorizing wine and more intent on enjoying it, appreciating how it flatters the snack platter we've made or simply the company we're in.

Also, it's best not to speak too soon when a bottle is opened: We are enjoying *living* wines. These wines change—even over the time it takes to drink them.

In natural wine, there's no set of terms you need to adhere to when tasting. For that reason, it's always welcome to use descriptors that are meaningful to you personally, rather than trying to emulate someone's standard. Your glass of Cabernet Franc might remind you of cotton candy you had at the state fair as a kid, and that's valid. The rosé blend is giving you Capri Sun vibes? Some people will identify with that, and some won't.

The process of tasting a natural wine involves engaging all your senses. First, examine the color and appearance of the wine. Pour into a simple, all-purpose glass with a stem, and lift it up to the light. Does it look like there was maceration? If so, was it for a long time or just briefly? Does the wine look light-bodied or medium-bodied? Put the glass on a table, grip the stem between your pointer finger and thumb, and gently swirl without lifting it up. This opens up the aromas.

---

\* *Somm*, Director Jason Wise, Forgotten Man Films, United States (2013).

Somm: An informal abbreviation of "sommelier," a person whose job it is to know and serve wine in a restaurant.

We've Got the Funk

Lift the glass to your nose and inhale. In a young wine, you may notice yeastiness—one hallmark of a wild fermentation. Keep swirling and sniffing, and see what else arrives to your olfactory system. You may notice fruity aromas (fresh or dried; red or dark), floral notes, outdoor fragrances like straw or rainforest, or whatever else comes to mind.

Take a small sip, and swish it around so it coats the insides of your mouth. Is the wine refreshing? Do the tannins linger on your tongue? Notice the texture: What does it tell you about the grape varieties in the wine, or the winemaking technique? Or what questions does the texture bring up?

A few basic descriptors are helpful when you're learning about natural wines and trying to connect what's in your glass with what happened in the vineyard or cellar. Try using the following terms as a guideline when you're tasting.

**FRUITY:** Most of us grew up hearing that wines could be dry or sweet, but this is a misleading distinction. A finished, bottled wine, unless it is indicated to be *demi-sec* (off-dry), is dry. If it weren't dry, it would re-ferment in the bottle. What the word "sweet" is meant to describe could be summarized as fruity. If you are perceiving "sweetness" in a wine, use the descriptor "fruity," because it better encapsulates flavors such as tropical, berry, or stone fruits. Fruity flavors might also indicate carbonic maceration (see p. 88).

**BRIGHT OR LIVELY:** Let's talk about acidity, a crucial component in wine. Acidity is what makes wine dance on your tongue; it tingles, even. Without acidity, a wine is flabby, heavy. Winemakers can achieve acidity by harvesting earlier or by adding tartaric or malic acid. We know which approach natural winemakers prefer! Generally, natural winemakers harvest quite early, because grapes are heathiest when they have just entered the ripeness window (before birds swoop in to damage them, or excessive sun or rain arrives). You may notice that natural wines have more acidity than conventional ones. Acidity appears as citrus fruit flavors and a bright, lively sensation on your palate.

**TANNIC:** Tannins are astringent polyphenols found primarily on grape skins and stems (and in many other plant foods) that impart flavor and texture into a wine when it undergoes skin contact during fermentation. Depending on the grape variety and the length and type of skin maceration, tannins might manifest on the palate as a grippy feeling, with notes of cranberry, blood orange, leather, or tobacco. Generally, tannins feel dry in the mouth—what people

# welcome to a Pandora's box: "Minerality" is a tasting note that some love to identify...

usually describe as a dry wine is often a tannic one; or they could be referring to the "crisp" character that many conventional wines achieve by arresting malolactic fermentation. Tannins usually develop complexity as a wine ages in bottle. Both whites and reds can be made with skin contact, leading to an array of tannin levels.

**MINERAL:** Welcome to a Pandora's box: "Minerality" is a tasting note that some love to identify, while others profess that it doesn't exist. When we talk about minerality, we're referring to the ways that a vineyard's rocks or soils make themselves known in a finished wine. Imagine the sensation of licking a rock: cold, chalky. Some people identify this characteristic in wines—especially wines from regions known for limestone, like Chablis or Burgundy, or the Muscadet region of the Loire, where vines grow on metamorphic rocks like gneiss. Minerality is considered positively, indicating that a wine displays terroir, finesse, and aging potential.

**FUNKY:** This is a popular term, but it's also a little vague. Funky notes could merely refer to the fact that the wine had a wild-yeast fermentation (think of sipping kombucha) or to a so-called flaw like *Brettanomyces*. Contrary to what many seem to think, not all natural wines are funky—it really depends on the grape variety and fermentation method. "Funky" could also indicate volatile acidity (see p. 136).

# NATURAL WINE & POTENTIAL FLAWS

There's a reason that enologists started adding commercial yeasts, acids, sulfites, and so on to wine in the first place: stability. These products ensure that a wine will turn out untransmutable and consistent, no matter what the vintage provides. A consistent wine is useful in a marketing sense. What's enticing about natural wines, however, is that they reflect the peculiarities of a certain year, telling a unique story about place and time, without any kind of veil to hide behind.

All wines are susceptible to flaws. But when wines are unfiltered and unsulfited, flaws are more likely. Thinking about flaws in natural wine, it helps to lean on the Japanese concept of *wabi-sabi*, which acknowledges imperfections found in nature.

You'll ultimately decide on your own personal thresholds for flaws in natural wines. The following are a few worth knowing about.

**VOLATILE ACIDITY (VA) AND ETHYL ACETATE (EA):** Fermenting grapes, left untended or with too much intensity, will develop vinegary qualities. In small amounts, volatile acidity adds character to a wine, but when the level grows very noticeable, the wine is unruly—too much like salad dressing—and it can even be illegal to export. Don't toss the bottle, though—high-VA wine works well for braising stews. Volatile acidity is easily confused with ethyl acetate, a related substance that manifests itself as nail-polish remover on the nose and palate.

**MOUSE, OR MOUSINESS:** If a high-pitched squeal came in the form of an unpleasant odor-taste sensation… Mouse is a colloquial term for a bacterial infection that occurs in low-sulfite or no-sulfite-added wines. It often happens when a wine is made or bottled too quickly, and it can also be related to high pH in the wine. As a drinker, you may taste mouse as a wet-cardboard or puppy's-breath note; it always reminds me of wet almonds. Not something you want in your glass. The good news is, when a bottled wine has mouse, it can recover and become mouse-free in a few months if stored in a cool place. Regardless, mousiness signals a structurally weak wine that, if drinkable at all, will need to be consumed cold and quickly.

**OXIDATION:** When a wine is exposed to oxygen, either during the fermentation and aging process or while in bottle (due to a bad cork), it can develop straw- or hay-like flavors and feel heavy on the tongue. Some producers deliberately produce oxidized wines, and certain styles (such as Sherry or traditional Jura whites) rely on it. Plenty of wine drinkers enjoy the flavor of oxidation. Perhaps oxidation is only a flaw when done in excess or accidentally. It can add personality to a wine when in balance with the overall profile.

**REDUCTION:** The opposite of oxidation, reduction occurs when a wine hasn't had enough oxygen contact. Characteristics of a reductive wine include struck-matchstick or rubbery notes. Reduction can occur if a wine is made only in stainless steel or fiberglass without any porosity, or from lees contact. As with oxidation, reduction isn't necessarily a flaw when it's balanced by other aspects of the wine.

Natural Wine & Potential Flaws

# natural wines reflect the peculiarities of a certain year...

**RE-FERMENTATION:** "Is this wine *meant* to be fizzy?" If you're not sure, then it's probably not. It will have been bottled with some accidental, residual sugar and is now re-fermenting. Handle with care, and serve cold. Alternatively, yeasts may have become active in the wine by some other means. It's alive in there! A re-fermenting bottle isn't ideal, but it might be drinkable. The problem could also be a result of how it was shipped or stored. If it's a *little* bit of spritz that quickly dissipates, don't worry—that's just residual carbon dioxide from fermentation.

**BRETTANOMYCES:** Both conventional and natural wines can be afflicted by this yeast strain that's affectionately called *Brett*. When these particular wild yeasts are present in a vineyard or winery, they can degrade wine phenols to the point where they develop aromas resembling barnyard, horse mane, or even gym socks. Interestingly, *Brett* flavors are common in older Bordeaux wines and considered an integral part of their profile. So, when is *Brett* too much and therefore a flaw? It's subjective but, in short, when the winemaker didn't intend it.

**CORK TAINT (TCA; 2,4,6-TRICHLOROANISOLE):**
A "corked" wine is a sad thing, because it's nobody's fault that the wine has been ruined. And it's also very prevalent. Up to 10 percent of wines that are closed with natural cork are infected with cork taint, or TCA, a chemical compound that gives a wine unpleasant metallic, mushroomy flavors. Unfortunately, the only way to discover that a wine has cork taint is by opening it. Some producers have grown tired enough of experiencing cork taint on their own wines that they've begun using alternative closures such as synthetic cork or glass stoppers.

# …telling a unique story about place and time, without any kind of veil to hide behind

# WHAT TO DO IF A WINE IS FLAWED

**In conventional wine culture, a flaw makes a wine totally undrinkable and unsellable. Within natural wine, we can be a little more forgiving.**

Have mercy when you encounter flaws in non-manipulated wines. The makers aren't *trying* to give you a faulty product. Sometimes, a wine is bottled and sold before it's ready. Often, the journey from the vineyard to a city where wines are sold can shake up bottles or heat them too much and cause them to misbehave—usually just temporarily. Trust that producers and importers are trying to learn from their mistakes. Nobody wants to release flawed wines. Even so, it happens: For every three or four stunning, life-changing wines, you will encounter five or six pretty good wines and, inevitably, one *not*-so-great bottle. The gamble is part of the pleasure.

Of course, it's difficult to identify a problem until you've poured and tasted a wine—and then it may be too late to decide not to purchase it! Here are some ways to approach a flawed wine.

* If you are sampling a wine in a restaurant and you detect a flaw before accepting the glass or bottle you've ordered, let the sommelier know so they can also check it. You do not have to accept the wine if you think something is wrong, and hopefully they'll offer you a bottle in better shape.

* If you notice a flaw when opening a bottle at home, you can try to take it back to the wine shop and request a refund. However, the wine will transform dramatically between opening it and your next trip to the shop, so it may be difficult for the shop to decide what to do. The shop will probably write it off as a loss, since they can't exactly send a half-full bottle back to a distributor or producer. If you bought the wine online, your chances of recompensation are very low: Shipping an opened wine seems unwise—if permissible at all.

* With wines that appear mousy, if you have multiple bottles from the same producer at home, simply tuck them away in a cool, dark place and check them again in six months to see if the mouse has dissipated. Feel free to alert the bottle shop to the problem so they can do the same.

* With wines that have high VA, perhaps you can enjoy them chilled. But if not, they make excellent cooking wine, especially for braised dishes.

* Try decanting a flawed wine to see if it helps the problems dissipate.

# the gamble is part of the pleasure

# SERVING TEMPERATURES & DECANTING

The conventional wisdom you've been told about how to serve wine? Well, it is perfect for... Conventional wines. When you're drinking artisanal and natural wine, the old rules are flipped on their heads. Let's look at how they apply to all the different categories of wines.

## WHITE

Except for an extremely hot day when you absolutely must crack open an ice-cold bottle, or if you're enjoying very spicy food, there is no need to drink white wines fresh out of the fridge. Serving them too cold blunts their aromas and flavors. Try taking white wine out of the fridge ten minutes before opening it, and don't feel compelled to put it on ice directly after pouring the first glass; you'll see how much stronger the aromas are.

## RED

We've talked about "light reds" in this book in several contexts: *glou-glou* wines, carbonic-maceration wines; low-alcohol blends… With all of these styles of red wine, you will enjoy your drink so much more if the bottle is chilled first. Put a light red on ice or in the fridge for 20 minutes, then open it directly—see how the tannins are lifted and the texture silky with that extra freshness. A medium- or full-bodied red can be served at room temperature unless you want to chill it for a more refreshing effect.

## ROSÉ

Forget ice-cold Provençal rosé, fine-tuned to deliver that signature pale pink color and filtered to death. Natural rosé is a more traditional

# the old rules are flipped on their heads

product, made similarly to red wine but with a shorter maceration time. These handcrafted rosés should be served closer to room temperature, not freezing-cold, to appreciate their complexities.

## ORANGE

With orange wines being white wines that are effectively made like a red, they vary from lightly macerated and acid-driven to intensely tannic and alcoholic. Keeping in mind the great diversity in this category, in general, opt to serve orange wines cool, but not too cold.

## SPARKLING

Any natural sparkling wine, whatever its production process, will benefit from being served very cold. Too warm, and the wine is guaranteed to explode when opened. Use a sparkling-wine stopper to retain the bubbles and put that bottle on ice between pours.

## TO DECANT OR NOT TO DECANT?

The purpose of a decanter is to oxygenate a wine. Often, decanting is used with heavily tannic wines like Sangiovese, especially when they are aged in oak barrels and then aged for years in bottles. Before decanting, the wine may seem clumsy or tight, or the tannins will be aggressive. With air, the flavors should integrate better.

Decanting can be useful for natural wines that, similarly, are made from potentially strong-flavored grape varieties such as Malvasia, Nero d'Avola, Cabernet Sauvignon, Tempranillo, Nebbiolo, or Savagnin. It's also particularly useful for aged wines in general: Anything ten years old or older could benefit from decanting.

Many natural wines, though, should not be decanted. One reason is that they are simply too delicate—decanting tends to devolve the flavor rather than improving it. However, if your wine seems a little reductive (see p. 137), or if it has a little residual carbon dioxide, decanting could help blow off these gases.

Ultimately, you'll use your own judgment. If a wine is known to be made from a sturdy variety, is higher in alcohol and tannin, and has aged in the bottle, it's probably a good candidate for decanting. Otherwise, it's best to pour straight into the glass.

# AGING & STORING NATURAL WINES

It was during the brief time that I was fortunate enough to "live" in Paris—if you count squatting on a friend's couch as living—that I collected proof of natural wine's aging potential. Many wine bars in Paris and throughout France have underground storage space where bottles can age peacefully, protected from heat and light. That's why Paris is one of the best places in the world to enjoy aged natural wines—along with Tokyo, where wines are stored in cool rooms.

It's important not to believe the myth that natural wine doesn't age properly or will go bad without sulfites. Nearly all natural wines benefit from age; the reason they are often drunk young is simply that many winemakers live paycheck to paycheck, so to speak, and therefore need to bottle within a year of fermentation in order to maintain cash flow. Most wine bars don't have the space to age the bottles, so typically what you get is something released within the past year.

If you can, please do age natural wines at home. You'll need to keep them someplace cool (around 55°F [13°C] is optimum) and away from sunlight. A closet will do. Under the bed will do. Generally, aging bottles on their sides is ideal, because the wine stays in contact with the cork and keeps it moist, so that the closure remains effective.

The optimum drinking window for natural wines is a funny thing to try to pin down. Because of the reasons described above, many producers wouldn't know specifically what the windows are. One approach would be to consider the grape varieties in the wines. Here are some varieties that are universally considered to have the best aging potential:

* Cabernet Sauvignon
* Chardonnay
* Gamay
* Malvasia
* Nebbiolo
* Pinot Noir
* Sangiovese
* Savagnin
* Syrah
* Tempranillo
* Touriga Nacional
* Trebbiano

This is not an absolute. Vineyard age, soil type, and exposition make a difference: A Chardonnay wine made from a very young plot on flat land in Anjou is not the same as a wine made

# it's important not to believe the myth that natural wine doesn't age properly

from 70-year-old Chardonnay vines grown on a highly prized Burgundy **cru**. Then there are regional styles that affect a wine's aging potential—Sauvignon Blanc from the Sancerre region, for example, is meant to mature, while that from New Zealand is generally for drinking young. Over time, you'll begin to understand how vineyard farming and the winemaking process reflect a wine's potential to age. Wines that age in ceramic and wood before bottling are considered more age-worthy than those made only in fiberglass or stainless steel.

**Cru: A vineyard of recognized quality, specifically in France.**

Aging natural wines allows their complexities to develop—and their faults, if they have any, to integrate into the overall beauty of the wine. If you can age multiple bottles of the same wine at home, you'll be able to observe how it changes over time. Just be sure the space isn't exposed to sun or too warm; the wines may re-ferment and push out their corks.

Sparkling wine, including pét-nat, is an excellent style to age. Aged sparkling wine takes on depth and complexity and is a very special drink to pair with rich dishes like fried chicken or seafood, creamy cheeses, fresh oysters, or umami/savory foods such as yakitori. Store fizz horizontally in a cool, dark spot, then chill fully before serving.

# EXPERT VIEW: THE ART OF PAIRING NATURAL WINES WITH FOOD

## WITH SOPHIE O'KANE, WINE DIRECTOR OF JULIE RESTAURANT, MELBOURNE

With fertile agricultural and viticultural regions just beyond the city, Melbourne, Australia, has one of the world's most exciting restaurant scenes. Dining in Melbourne means fresh ingredients and handcrafted wines from near and far. Since its opening in 2023, in a former convent, Julie Restaurant has taken farm-to-table one step further, with a menu based largely on its own tiny plot of no-till veggies and herbs mere steps from the kitchen. After trying an amazing meal of charred octopus with fizzy red wine at Julie, I asked wine director Sophie O'Kane—who previously worked at Manzé, a creative Mauritian-influenced restaurant pouring natural wines—to weigh in on the art of pairing.

**HOW DID YOU WIND UP AS A NATURAL WINE SOMMELIER?**
Before wine became my career, I was working in health care, but in my spare time I loved exploring new expressions of wine that often refused to play by "the rules." It was refreshing for me because it was inclusive and approachable—not stuffy. The people I encountered in those early days were encouraging, lovely. They didn't make wine seem inaccessible and scary. During Covid, I went through a reassessment, and this led me to explore being a sommelier.

I became friends with [Manzé's chef-owner] Nagesh Seethiah through a distribution role. He was pouring wines that were edgy, wines that wouldn't pair with typical European food. The other thing that appealed to me about Manzé was that the wine list really embraced diversity and inclusivity. It featured winemakers that represent all parts of society: people of color, LGBTQ, women, family-run businesses. That resonated with me as a female in a classically very male-dominated industry.

**WHAT WAS THE MENU LIKE AT MANZÉ, AND HOW DID YOU PAIR NATURAL WINES WITH THE FOOD?**
Nagesh's Mauritian food is a nod to the food of his childhood, which was

# my challenge was to pick a wine that complements and can stand up to the huge flavor of the charred octopus

largely Indian-Mauritian, with an eye on seasonality through pickling and preserving. The food is spicy but not necessarily hot, with incredible depth and complexity.

One of the Manzé staples is a fried taro ball with ginger and spring onion. It's crispy on the outside, savory and more-ish, and it's served with this incredible hot sauce made with preserved ingredients. With this dish, you could go for aromatic varieties like Muscat, Gewurztraminer, or Ugni Blanc.

**THERE WERE USUALLY A FEW SEAFOOD DISHES ON THE MENU AT MANZÉ, JUST AS THERE ARE AT JULIE, WHERE YOU WORK NOW. CAN YOU TALK ABOUT HOW YOU PAIR WINES WITH SEAFOOD?**
At both Manzé and Julie, we had an octopus dish on the menu. Octopus can be tricky to pair with wine because of its strong flavor, which can also depend on how it's cooked.

At Manzé, there was a dish that was seasoned with octopus bits that had been fermented with aromatics and spices. It was very punchy. For the pairing, I went with a red blend called La Route des Crêtes, from Catherine Bernard in the Languedoc. She makes only red wines but prefers to drink whites. This was a blend of Grenache, Mourvèdre, Marselan, and Cinsault—bold, rich, opulent varieties—but she doesn't make it like a big red wine.

In contrast, at Julie, the octopus is poached until tender, then charred and served with tomatoes, onions, and herbs from the garden. My challenge was to pick a wine that complements and can stand up to the huge flavor of the charred octopus. I've started pouring an Australian Lambrusco [a sparkling red, originally from the Emilia-Romagna region of Italy] from Babche Wines. This particular Lambrusco has a very gentle bubble that acts like a palate cleanser with each sip. In summer, it's very fitting. The actual flavor profile of the wine

is very earthy, while the bubble brings up acidity, and it goes so well with this preparation of octopus.

There was also an octopus ragù at Julie, served over *anelli* pasta. For the ragù, I went with an extended-maceration white wine. Originally, it was a wine from Federico Orsi. Then I was pouring the Jakot from Dario Prinčič.

**WHY DID AN EXTENDED-MACERATION (SKIN-CONTACT) WINE WORK SO WELL WITH THE RAGÙ?**
It needs a wine with tannin and texture. This could be a red, but that feels too obvious, so I chose a macerated white wine. The Jakot is made of the aromatic Friulano variety, which has stone-fruit flavors that give it lightness. It is macerated for several weeks. This maceration lends the wine tannin, structure, and texture.

**HOW DO YOU LIKE TO SERVE MACERATED WHITES?**
I would serve the wine cold and let it develop in the glass. When a wine is too cold, it dampens the fruit and amplifies the acid. Once the temperature comes up, you get a better balance of fruit, acid, and tannin. Also, there's the exposure to oxygen in your glass or in the open bottle, and you'll see the wine change—the integration of all the components of the wine.

**WHAT'S A TRIED-AND-TRUE PHILOSOPHY YOU RELY ON WHEN PAIRING NATURAL WINES WITH FOOD?**
There are two ways you can approach pairing a beverage to your food. The drink can either complement the flavors that are already detectable in the dish, or it can act as a contrast, meaning it provides a counterbalance to the flavors or textures in the dish.

One of my favorite pairings ever is mortadella and Riesling. The acid of the wine cuts through the fatty mortadella—they're opposites, which makes it work.

"Grows together, goes together" works, too. Research the region, and see what people eat and drink there. A classic example is goat cheese and Sauvignon Blanc, both from the Loire Valley in France.

I also like to think about temperature and texture with a wine pairing. Is it going to be jarring to sip a crisp aromatic white wine after a mouthful of Irish beef stew?

**AT WHAT POINT DO YOU DEVIATE FROM THE RULES? WHERE DOES CREATIVITY COME IN?**
Understanding the rules of pairing is helpful because you can then choose to break them. If you understand that it's the acid in the Riesling and how its texture coats your palate, working with the fat of the mortadella, and that this is why it tastes so good, then you can essentially trust your palate.

Ask yourself, What are the flavors I love that make this dish amazing and that I want to showcase? Then you can go backward from there and pick a wine that might not be traditional but still works in the same way.

**WHEN YOU ARE LOOKING AT A MENU AND THINKING ABOUT WHICH NATURAL WINES TO PAIR, HOW DO YOUR THOUGHTS PROCEED?**
I always ask my dining companions or the guests in my restaurant what kinds of wines they normally like to drink. Depending on what they say, I can pick out a feature of that style or variety of wine that I know is present in a wine on the list. As much as we can get super-finicky about how to pair wines, you've got to like what you're drinking. My mum doesn't like white wine, for example, so no matter how amazing the pairing is, she'd always prefer a red alternative. I believe this is almost always possible—there's a red and a white option to go with most things.

# PERFECT PAIRINGS YOU MUST TRY

## COMTÉ & MACVIN

The nutty flavors and firm texture of Comté cheese from the Jura pair beautifully with the similar characteristics found in Macvin, a unique, long-aged Jura wine made from fresh unfermented grape must with spirit added. Domaine de l'Octavin has a Macvin-style wine from 2011; it's a rare bird but worth the hunt. Another option is the Pinot Noir-based Macvin from Bénédicte and Stéphane Tissot. This pairing is a stunning way to finish a meal.

## PIZZA & SANGIOVESE

A perfectly crisp and tart sourdough crust, topped with melted *fior di latte* cheese and a few heavenly anchovies, deserves a good wine. Look for a red wine based on Sangiovese, a grape grown throughout central Italian regions like Tuscany, Umbria, and Lazio, and you've found the match: The grape's rustic, earthy notes are flattered by the variety's potential for acidity, bringing out the fermented notes in the pizza dough and cheese and the salinity of any toppings. Choose a Sangiovese with slightly lower ABV (12.5% or below) to ensure the wine will have acidity.

## FRIED CHICKEN & PÉT-NAT

With rich salty, spicy food like fried chicken, your best bet is a perfectly cold, fizzy wine. It's well known that bubbles and acidity work together to cut through the fat and richness of fried food. Like it spicy? Slather on that mayo-sriracha sauce—the fizzy wine will calm down the tingling on your tongue, each sip leaving you wanting more.

## OSSO BUCO & A SKIN-CONTACT WHITE FROM FRIULI OR GEORGIA

In winter, I love preparing a big pot of braised meat—osso buco (veal shank) is my choice cut. The dish requires a full-bodied, tannic wine, but let's think outside the box. Go for a macerated white from Friuli (northeastern Italy) or from the Republic of Georgia, two regions where producers are known for making white wine in a more powerful style—stronger flavors alongside nice acidity. A long-macerated white wine from either Friuli or Georgia, served lightly-chilled alongside the piping-hot stew, will keep your palate from being overburdened while flattering the rich flavors of the braised meat.

# NOT SO GOOD: PAIRINGS TO AVOID

Certain flavors really rub each other the wrong way. Here's a list of pairings to avoid—and how to find something better to drink.

## ARTICHOKES & ANYTHING

Your favorite spring produce is full of a compound called cynarin that can make wine taste metallic. Why not try a delicious, naturally made cider instead of wine? Whether it's made exclusively from apples or pears or from a combination of apples, pears, and quince, a handmade cider is an excellent way to wash down a light veggie dish like grilled or marinated artichokes. La Cidrerie du Vulcain is a Swiss cider producer working in a natural way, with ciders made sparkling by adding juice before bottling. Many natural winemakers also have a cider in their range; it's your chance to see what your favorite producers can do with apples.

## CHOCOLATE & RED WINE

Even the darkest of dark chocolates cannot make this work. The tannins of red wine and those in chocolate clash profoundly. Whisky or grappa would be a better choice here, but if it needs to be wine, go for a zero- or low-*dosage* grower Champagne. This advice applies to ice cream, too, and any dessert made primarily with chocolate or cream (cheesecake, panna cotta, chocolate cake, tiramisu)—it's just not a wine-pairing situation.

## MEXICAN FOOD & OAKY CHARDONNAY

If you're enjoying a meal of tacos or *mole*, don't ruin the delicate balance of flavors with an overpowering, rich white wine. Not all Chardonnay is buttery and oaky. If you can find one made in ceramic or stainless steel, you'll be fine—a mineral, light Chardonnay would work with Mexican or Tex-Mex cuisine. Even better: beer. Some foods seem destined to be paired with non-grape beverages.

## EAST ASIAN OR CHINESE CUISINE & HEAVY RED WINE

The gorgeous lemongrass, basil, chili, and mint flavors of Thai or Vietnamese cuisine, as well as the earthy, umami, peppercorn flavors that dominate many Mandarin and Cantonese dishes, will either disappear under the heavy tannin and fruit notes of wines like Syrah or Cabernet Sauvignon, or they will battle unpleasantly on your tongue. If you must have a red wine, try a light, bouncy red like Cabernet Franc or Gamay—or better yet, opt for a white wine: either one made with skin contact or an aromatic variety like Riesling, Malvasia, or Gewurztraminer.

# HOSTING A NATURAL WINE-FORWARD GATHERING

I've created a sample menu that I would serve at my dream dinner party, which you can use to inspire your own gatherings for natural wine lovers. Use it as a template or inspiration—you can swap or skip parts based on your vision for the evening (or your budget or dietary preferences).

When considering your own menu, just for fun, try to think first of wines you'd like to serve, then ask yourself what dishes would flatter them. Or consider the wines and dishes together.

Ultimately, it doesn't matter if you get each pairing "right" or if one wine is slightly warmer than it should be; the point is to discover new natural wines with friends over great food and conversation.

## GLASSWARE & SET-UP

If you've got flutes and absolutely love them, feel free to use them—but they aren't better glassware. A flute preserves bubbles so they last longer in the glass, but it mutes the flavor of the wine itself. A regular, all-purpose glass is ideal for sparkling wine made in the style of pét-nat. Remember: These are handmade wines in which the bubbles are integrated into the wine itself, not meant to overpower.

Choosing an all-purpose glass also means that you can allow guests to keep one glass throughout the evening. Consider putting out a Sharpie on your counter and allowing guests to write their initials or a cute drawing on the base of the glass (a surprisingly good icebreaker). Or invest in a set of dangly wine-glass charms that sit on the base to help guests hang onto their glasses.

Alternatively, tumblers are totally fine if you're serving fairly simple wines. They won't allow you to swirl the glass and bring out the aromas fully, but there's something very cute about sipping out of vintage-looking tumblers at a dinner party. It de-emphasizes the wine and puts the focus on the food and conversation.

To improve the flow of the evening, put out two small pitchers: one with tap water, for rinsing out glasses between servings, and another for dumping. Show guests that they can simply pour a little water into their glass and swirl it around, then dump it, between trying different wines.

Put some water on the table, too— you don't want people getting too tipsy or dehydrated, which is easy to do when you're serving one fantastic wine after another.

# WELCOME DRINKS

When your guests arrive, don't make them stand around holding an umbrella, meeting your neighbor for the first time. They should be able to drop their things and receive a drink straightaway.

To accompany your welcome drinks, you may want to have a few dishes of marinated olives sitting out; if it's a colder night, consider briefly warming them in a pan. A bowl of roasted almonds is also ideal.

### INGREDIENTS

- 2 parts any bitter aperitivo (Campari or Cynar or something artisanal like Forthave Spirits' Red or Chinati Vergano's Americano)
- 3 parts your choice of pét-nat (white, skin-contact, or rosé)
- Splash of soda water
- Citrus, a sprig of thyme, or a green olive on a toothpick, to garnish

## MY PÉT-NAT SPRITZ

This is the perfect opportunity to serve a pét-nat spritz. Typically, a spritz is made with some kind of aperitivo drink such as Aperol (a sweeter choice) or Campari (more bitter), plus Prosecco. But you can vary it any way you want, and using quality pét-nat instead of Prosecco makes a giant difference.

I swear by my pét-nat spritz and think that once you've tried it, you'll never go back to using Prosecco in your spritzes. Have your ice in a chilled metal bowl, glassware (a lowball glass or a regular wine glass) and garnishes and your choice of aperitivo ready, and your sparkling wine in the fridge or resting in a bucket of ice.

This drink is perfect for a warm spring evening or a cool autumn afternoon. It takes about two minutes to make and is visually impressive. I've written it in terms of ratios. You can use a cocktail jigger to measure one standard part.

### METHOD

Pour the aperitif and sparkling wine over ice in a tall glass, then add the soda water. Decorate the glass with your chosen garnish, and serve with potato chips, olives, or cheese.

# PURE BUBBLES

Keeping it simple? Bubbles are designed to whet our appetites, calm our nerves, and ease us into a situation. One tip: Stock up on a few sparkling-wine stoppers, which you can order online. They keep the bubbles inside the bottle but won't go flying up to the ceiling like a regular cork would. The following are naturally sparkling wines that make excellent welcome drinks.

## COSTADILÀ MÓZ

This is a *col fondo* from an iconic sparkling wine project in the Veneto. Móz is a blend of Glera (the main Prosecco grape) and a local variety called Moscato Fior d'Arancio. If you can't find this exact cuvée, anything from Costadilà will be a hit. Some of the cuvées are labeled according to the elevation of the vineyard it comes from—if you can get the whole lineup, you could study how elevation affects a wine's flavor profile. How's that for a convo starter? Low ABV, too (10.5%), to help your guests start slow.

## DOMAINE MOSSE MOUSSAMOUSSETTES

One of my all-time favorite wines—and one I had the privilege of observing in process when I picked grapes for the Mosse family during the 2017 vintage. A gorgeous sparkling rosé with strong bubbles, this is made of Loire Valley red varieties including Pineau d'Aunis, Cabernet Franc, and Grolleau. It is bottled under Champagne cork (unlike most pét-nats, which are topped with a crown cap) to allow more oxygen into the wine as it ages in bottle. A stellar sparkling.

## MILAN NESTAREC DANGER 380 VOLTS

I'm a huge fan of all the Nestarec wines, made in eastern Czechia, and this one is no exception. It's a lively white bubbly made from a vineyard where hybrid grape Neuburger, Müller-Thurgau (a cross between Riesling and a table grape called Madeleine Royale), and Muscat grow together. Refreshing and bright.

## OYSTER RIVER WINEGROWERS MORPHOS

Made in Maine, this is a newly classic American natural wine. Oyster River farms vineyards locally and also bring grapes from Upstate New York to their MidCoast winery. The Morphos white is a blend of Cayuga and Seyval, two cold-hardy varieties, while the rosé is Merlot. Both are fruity and delicious. Oyster River also makes a wine called Chaos, a very elegant traditional-method sparkling with two fermentations, as done in Champagne. It's a must-try, perfect for impressing your guests.

## THE OTHER RIGHT BRIGHT YOUNG THING

This Adelaide Hills sparkling light red from Alex Schulkin (see p. 111 for his Expert View on sulfites) is a hit with or without food. It's made from Pinot Noir and Chardonnay for that baby-Champagne vibe. With tannin and crunch from the red grapes, this wine has a nice grip and heft to complement the lightness of the bubbles.

# FIRST COURSE: BUTTERNUT SQUASH SOUP

Soup is such a nice starter at a dinner party. You can prepare it entirely in advance, and it gives the house a beautiful, welcoming aroma.

My older brother always makes butternut squash soup for family gatherings in autumn. Below is his recipe. Serves 6.

### INGREDIENTS

2 butternut squashes, halved vertically and seeds removed
oil, for drizzling
3 garlic cloves, chopped
1 onion or 2 shallots, chopped
knob of ginger, chopped
1 liter (4½ cups) stock (chicken or veggie)
110ml (½ cup) cream
ground nutmeg, cinnamon, and chili (to taste)
salt and pepper

### TO GARNISH

crispy fried sage leaves
pumpkin seeds

### METHOD

Preheat the oven to 200°C (400°F). Drizzle the squash halves with olive oil, season with salt and pepper and place them skin-side down in a roasting tray. Roast for about 45 minutes, until they are soft enough for a fork to go through with little resistance. Allow to cool, then peel off the skins and cut into chunks.

In a large, deep pan, heat a drizzle of oil and sauté the garlic with the onion or shallots, stirring constantly, until translucent. Add the squash and the ginger to the garlic and onion, and sauté for around 3 minutes. Stir in the stock and then the cream. Use an immersion blender to blend until creamy, then add nutmeg, cinnamon and chili, as you like. Season with salt and pepper.

Finish with crispy fried sage leaves, pumpkin seeds and a drizzle of oilve oil.

## PAIRING

Entice your guests to join you in the kitchen while you stir the soup by opening a delicious wine, then pour it again at the table. Gazzetta's Bianco Trilli is a mesmerizing skin-contact blend of Vermentino, Malvasia, Trebbiano, and Ansonica from the Lazio/Umbria area of Italy. Made with aromatic grapes, it harmonizes well with roasted flavors and has the acidity to cut through creaminess in a dish.

You could also consider the following wines:
* From Spain, Esmeralda García's Verdejo wines made in Castilla y León—unctuous and full-bodied, with earthy, mineral depth;
* Medium-bodied, mineral Italian whites from Cascina degli Ulivi, Cascina 'Tavijn, or Alessandro Viola—a perfect pairing;
* A Chardonnay from Burgundy or the Jura, like a barrel-aged Bourgogne Blanc from Fanny Sabre or an estate-bottled Ganevat;
* Matassa's aromatic, textured Cuvée Marguerite—ideal here.

# SECOND COURSE:
# CARBO-CREMA WITH RIGATONI ALLA VILLANA

When I first visited the gorgeous Italian vineyard of La Villana, overlooking Lake Bolsena in northern Lazio, winemaker Joy Kull's husband Simone made carbonara, the famous Roman pasta with guanciale and egg. I hung out in the kitchen slyly watching Simone as he prepared the elements, and years later I got the full recipe from him. Generally, in Rome, this dish is served with long pasta like spaghetti or bucatini, but in northern Lazio they like it with rigatoni.

Simone calls his version "carbo-crema" because he insists that the trick is making a creamy sauce in a blender. Serves 4.

## PAIRING

When Simone made this carbo-crema for us, we had it with Joy's La Villana *rosato*, made of the local red grape Aleatico, grown on volcanic soils. With just 24 hours of maceration, the wine was super-light, with aromas of cherry and roses, but also flavorful and tart enough to cut through the fat of the dish.

You could also consider the following wines:
* Another gorgeous rosé, such as Alessandro Viola's Nerello Mascalese with a touch of Nero d'Avola—full of minerality and energy, it's perfect with creamy pasta on a warm day;
* Domaine de l'Octavin's Elle Aime, a perfect example of natural wine's creative bent—mostly Pinot Noir with one-third Chardonnay from the same vineyard, this is a unique, ethereal drink, with bright fruit notes and a lash of Jura minerality;
* Martha Stoumen's "New American"-style Benchlands—a savory, refreshing, light red-and-white co-fermentation of **dry-farmed** vineyards featuring unlikely California heroes like Petit Sirah, Carignan, Colombard, Nero d'Avola, and others;
* Noir de Florette from Lucy M Wines—a racy, bright Pinot Noir made with carbonic maceration; its crushed-rose notes will flatter the earthy tones of the guanciale.

**Dry-farmed:** Non-irrigated vineyards; generally considered a mark of quality.

### INGREDIENTS

1 tablespoon olive oil
150–200g (5–7oz) guanciale (cured pork jowl—find it at an Italian grocer), cut into strips
½ shallot or pink onion (preferably Tropea, if you can find that variety), very finely sliced
6 eggs, separated
250g (9oz) freshly grated Pecorino cheese (the sweeter Tuscan kind, if you can find it, or the Roman kind, which is more common), plus extra to serve
400g (14oz) rigatoni
cracked black pepper
salt

In general, you'll want around 100g (3½oz) of pasta per person, ideally slow-dried pasta, which is better for digestion.

You'll need a stick blender or blender, a pot with a lid, and a trusty skillet or frying pan.

### METHOD

Heat the oil in a frying pan over a medium-high heat, then add the guanciale and shallot. Cook, stirring, until the guanciale renders and crisps—about 10 minutes. Let it cool.

Take a tablespoon of the cooled liquid fat and put it in a blender with 6 egg yolks and 1 egg white. Add the Pecorino and blitz until the whole thing gets creamy—2–3 minutes. Season with freshly cracked black pepper, then transfer to a non-reactive bowl.

Meanwhile, boil a large pot of lightly salted water for your rigatoni, and cook the pasta in the boiling water for 1 minute less than the official cooking time, at which point you should turn the heat back on to medium-high under the guanciale pan.

Reserving the pasta water, drain the rigatoni from the pot and add to the guanciale pan. Sauté for 1 minute with a tablespoon of the pasta water. Add the contents of the pan to the bowl with the egg-Pecorino mixture, while stirring. Serve immediately with extra grated Pecorino.

# AFTER DINNER:
# CHEESE PLATTER

**Ask your local cheesemonger for the following after-dinner cheeses or something similar.**

* An aged Comté—firm cow's-milk cheese from the Jura region with a nutty flavor;
* Gorgonzola dolce—creamy Italian blue cheese with a delicate sweetness;
* Manchego—crumbly sheep's cheese from Spain.

Arrange the cheeses on a plate with a different knife for each wedge, surrounded by a cluster of fresh and roasted nuts, and dried fruits. If your meal has been on the light side, perhaps add a slice of quince paste or fig compote and a smattering of lavosh—but don't be afraid to let the cheese stand alone.

## PAIRING

All of these post-meal cheeses will happily blend with an earthy, tannic, medium- or full-bodied red. The grippy texture of the wine will harmonize with the strong flavors of the cheese.

* Partida Creus's Vinel-lo is a rustic, crunchy-fruited blend of seven local varieties from the Penedès area of Catalonia, Spain. At only 10.5% ABV but full of flavor and with a kiss of tannin, it's a perfect wine to carry on conversation past dinner.
* Spring for a bottle of Ganevat's Trousseau/Poulsard, and let the earthy, fruity flavors of the wine play with the similar flavors in the cheeses.
* The enticing, brambly Bandita—Cascina 'Tavijn's wine made of the unsung red grape Barbera from Italy's Piedmont region—is a delightful wine whose acidity and perfume will flatter any dish, but especially cheese.

# AFTER DINNER:
# SWEET DESSERT

## PAIRING

The Piedmont vermouth producer Chinati Vergano makes several traditional herbal liqueurs, including its savory, tannic, cardamom-and-quinine-based Chinato, based on wine from the Barbaresco hills.

You could also consider the following options:
* A digestif liqueur from Faccia Brutto, based in Brooklyn, NY;
* An amaro from the Australian label Saison—unbelievable flavors in the range, including blackcurrant leaf.

For anything with sugar, you'll find that serving regular wine creates a muddled sensation on the palate. But a fortified wine flatters the textures and ingredients of a sweet dessert. Look for an amaro: this Italian herbal liqueur features botanicals such as wormwood, anise, and cinnamon, which promote digestion and relaxation.

# be confident about the wines you've chosen

**A HOSTING NOTE**

Your guests will obviously want to bring something to share at the dinner. But if you have carefully planned the wine pairings, their generous offerings may not fit. Don't feel the need to serve the wine they've brought; explain that you're looking forward to enjoying it, then tuck it away. Be confident about the wines you've chosen, and your guests will appreciate your artistry.

If you do want to incorporate your guests' wines (if only for budgetary reasons), why not let them know exactly what gaps you'd like to fill? You are actually doing them a favor if you tell them specifically to bring a pét-nat or a light red wine. (You can even suggest producers in this book.) Then the dinner becomes more of a playful episode where you and your guests experience the pairings together for the first time.

Choosing, Pouring, Enjoying

# MAKING WINE MEMORIES

Your friends will love the wines and want to know more. Place each empty bottle on your windowsill or on a separate table, so you can reflect on the lineup as the night goes on, and your guests can spend a moment checking out the bottle or photographing the label for future reference.

## DINNER PARTY FAVES

Use this space to jot down your wine memories from the night.

WINE NAME:

___

STYLE:

___

WHO CHOSE IT:

___

PAIRED WITH:

___

# GOING DEEPER

# DESTINATION NATURAL WINE BARS

Some travel for art, some for food, and some for natural wine. If the latter is you, take note of the bars and restaurants listed here. These are places that have attracted cult followings, won awards, and impressed the pants off me personally for their exceptional approach to natural wine. In these kinds of bars, you won't just find a perfect by-the-glass list; they also have full wine lists devoted to natural wine, and probably some semi-secret, hard-to-find bottles you might get access to if you ask nicely. All of these places have close connections with producers—you might even catch a tasting or run into a winemaker enjoying an off-duty drink on a trade visit. Consider this your natural wine-bar bucket list.

## EUROPE
40 Maltby Street – London, UK
Brawn – London, UK
Sager + Wilde — London, UK
Le Verre Volé – Paris, France
Septime La Cave – Paris, France
Aux Crieurs de Vin – Troyes, France
Bar Brutal – Barcelona, Spain
Bar Cortijo – Tarragona, Spain
Solovino – Rome, Italy
Enoteca Naturale – Milan, Italy
Vineria Sonora – Florence, Italy
Cave Ox – Solicchiata, Sicily, Italy
Vino Vero – Venice, Italy
Ved Stranden 10 – Copenhagen, Denmark

## US & CANADA
The Four Horsemen – New York City
The Ten Bells – New York City
Wildair – New York City
Botanica – Los Angeles, California
Ordinaire – Oakland, California
Rebel Rebel – Somerville, Massachusetts
Le Vin Papillon – Montréal, Quebec, Canada

## ASIA & OCEANIA
Ahiru Store – Tokyo, Japan
10 William St – Sydney, Australia
Waxflower – Melbourne, Australia

# NATURAL WINE FAIRS AROUND THE WORLD

You've finally finagled two weeks off work and found cheap tickets to Paris for February. That's right—you're heading to the world's most famous wine fair, La Dive Bouteille, for four full days of wine tasting with the greats and novices of the natural wine world.

How do you prepare? What to say when you finally stand before Vincent Laval and he pours you one of his Champagnes, in all its handmade glory, the bubbles profoundly integrated into an expression of terroir, and he looks at you to see what you think? It's a beautiful moment when this happens and one you won't easily forget.

Throughout the year, there are numerous natural wine tastings that are open to the public through ticketed admissions. These take place all around the world, with wine producers traveling to present their latest releases in person. Attending a natural wine fair is the perfect opportunity to develop your palate and learn. Tasting with the producer, you can ask questions about farming or vinification or clear up anything you're confused on. These fairs are also good fun and a great opportunity to meet other natural wine lovers or professionals. Each fair has its own criteria for selecting producers, and you can usually find that information on the event's website.

Below is a list of some of the longest-standing, most prominent, and exciting natural wine fairs around the world, with some basic details to help get you there. In general, most of these fairs offer different rates for trade and public; often there are separate time slots for exclusive trade access. You may be asked to provide proof of industry employment to receive the trade rate.

When you arrive, take it easy; you don't want to be the person who gets drunk early in the day. It's best to spit, not drink, every single wine—maybe practice spitting into a jug at home so your aim is fine-tuned. Reserve your swallowing for the wines you couldn't bear to spit—the really good sparklings, the elegant Pinots, the single-vineyard bottlings. Taste calmly and thoughtfully, taking notes (and offering the winemakers your praise as you taste) while also remembering to have water and food. You want to get through the day with recollection of what you enjoyed and who you met. There will be time to let loose later, at the after-party.

# attending a natural wine fair is the perfect opportunity to develop your palate and learn

## LA DIVE BOUTEILLE

This annual Loire Valley natural wine event was first held in 1999 and takes place over three days at the start of February. It is unbeatable as an experience. Picture tasting with some of the best-known natural wine producers in a giant limestone cave, with salty, fresh oysters for breakfast. Although La Dive, as it is affectionately known, originally focused on French producers, it has since expanded its international section, so you can taste natural wines from Italy, Spain, California, and beyond. Over time, other fairs have popped up in the region around the same point in the year, including the Salon St-Jean, which features biodynamic wineries, as well as off-salons curated by winemakers and their circle of friends. The wonderful result is that you can attend numerous fairs in the same area. La Dive and these other salons are geared toward professionals, but they are also open to the general public; the entry fee is minimal, and you can pay in cash at the entrance. There are shuttles from the Saumur train station to the Dive location itself, Caves Ackerman, but you'll want a car to explore the other salons in the area. It's a bit like the Cannes of the natural wine world: At the end of the day, all the winemakers meet at their favorite bistros and pass bottles around.
www.dive-bouteille.fr

## RAW WINE

The brainchild of Master of Wine and natural wine advocate Isabelle Legeron, this sizable one- or two-day tasting was founded in London in 2012 but now has iterations around the globe, including in New York, Los Angeles, Montréal, Paris, Copenhagen, Berlin, Shanghai, and Tokyo. In addition to a tasting, Raw Wine hosts "speakers' corners" during their fairs to encourage debate, discussion, and learning. Raw Wine's criteria for producers include organic farming at a minimum and no more than 50ppm of sulfite additions. Raw Wine is also notable in its push for transparency: Every producer's farming and winemaking is described in detail on the website.

www.rawwine.com/fairs

## BRUMAIRE

Since 2016, a cluster of friends in the California natural wine industry have organized Brumaire every March in the Bay Area, with the current venue being the Les Lunes winery. Brumaire is an extremely well-curated event, with no more than 40 producers invited, half from California and half from elsewhere. Ticket sales are announced on Brumaire's Instagram page and sold via an online platform. Get in quick, because spaces are limited—and you won't want to miss the legendary after-party at Ordinaire.

instagram.com/brumairesf

## AUGUSTA

If you needed an excuse to visit the stylish, historic Piedmontese city of Turin, in Italy, this Europe-focused natural wine fair and cultural event is for you. Established in 2023, the now-annual Augusta—named for *Augusta Taurinorum*, the ancient Roman settlement that gave birth to the city of Turin—takes place over two days in November, hosted by the venue Bunker, an eclectic cultural hub with both indoor and outdoor spaces.

You'll find producers of wine, cider, and beer from across Europe, along with food trucks, coffee stands, and a farmers' market. If the branding looks familiar, that's because natural wine pop artist Gianluca Cannizzo is one of the Augusta organizers. Buy tickets on the event website or at the door.

www.augustafieravino.com

## KARAKTERRE

The leading festival of central and Eastern European organic, biodynamic, and natural wines, Karakterre emerged as Austria's unmissable annual wine event. It has even launched a highly successful New York edition held at the Rockefeller Center. If you love Grüner Veltliner and Blaufränkisch, this fair is for you. The New York event takes place in autumn, while the Austrian iteration (in Eisenstadt, an hour outside of Vienna) happens in May. The Austrian edition is a two-day affair, and the New York one takes place across a single day. Both fairs are complemented by a series of themed side events organized by the trade community in restaurants, bistros, bars, wine shops, and clubs. Austrian tickets go on sale in February; New York tickets, in August. Your admission fee includes an official Karakterre Zalto glass, made in Austria.

www.karakterre.com

## PURA SEDE

Lisbon has become an intriguing place for natural wines, and this fair—a collaboration between an importer and a retailer—launched in 2020 as the first to celebrate the category in a public way. Alongside an extensive array of natural wine producers from Portugal itself, other European and even New World wineries also show up. You'll find wineries here that don't usually present at the bigger fairs. Held over a weekend in March, Pura Sede is a manageable size but growing each year, so grab your ticket in advance.

www.purasedelisboa.com

## ORANGE GLOU FAIR

When New York sommelier Doreen Winkler discovered orange wine, she fell in love so deeply that she devoted her entire career to this quirky yet diverse genre. Now she runs New York's annual Orange Glou Fair in late autumn. Expect hundreds of producers from around the world presenting their naturally made orange wines.

www.orangegloufair.com

## ZERO COMPROMISE

Each May, the Georgian capital of Tbilisi hosts one of the world's most exciting wine fairs, featuring natural winemakers from around the world. The two-day event is open to the public on both days. Georgian restaurants offer food, and there is generally an after-party at Vino Underground wine bar. Expect polyphonic singing.

## OTHER NOTABLE WINE FAIRS

* H2O Vegetal (Tarragona, Spain; annual)
* Solo Uva (Linguaglossa, Sicily, Italy; annual)
* The Wild Bunch (Portland, Oregon, USA; annual)
* Third Coast Soif (Chicago, Illinois, USA; annual)
* Maine Wild Wine Fest (Freeport, Maine, USA; annual)

# A HARVEST EXPERIENCE: WHAT TO KNOW

It's an exhilarating experience to join a winemaker for the annual harvest, and it's also a privilege. Consider that it's a very busy time for a winemaker, and they are taking you on regardless of your experience level. Be prepared to sleep and eat communally, wake at dawn and work until dusk, and do menial tasks such as picking grapes and washing buckets.

In France, working a grape harvest is a rite of passage for some high-school graduates. It helps them understand the seasonality of agriculture; provides them with a fun, stress-free work experience (for about €10 per hour); and is good physical activity. It can be all of this for you, too—and it's a great way to learn natural wine from within. There is no comparison between reading about fermentation while sitting in your living room in Philly versus digging into a vat of fermenting grapes and transferring them to a press. Once you've had the sensorial experience of a harvest, you'll know how wine is made at a profound level.

There are other times when you can gain work experience at a winery, such as winter vine pruning or spring bottling. Those are also times when a producer would be less busy and have more time to share knowledge with you. But there's nothing quite as special and memorable as a harvest

A Harvest Experience

# there's nothing quite as special and memorable as a harvest experience

experience. Here is some advice if you're thinking about heading to a winery to get your hands dirty.

* Contact a producer whose wines you love—and, if possible, ask your local wine shop (or the producer's importer or anyone you can) for an introduction, to improve your chances of a response.

* Follow up if they don't reply. Try sending a message or calling.

* Be very specific about what work you'd like to do and if you have any relevant experience. If you want to be in the winery and you've used a forklift before, mention that. But if your only experience is drinking their wines, be honest about that, and understand that they are taking you on in a spirit of generosity. Regardless, be prepared to do all the most basic jobs.

* Consider your timing. Southern-hemisphere harvests usually start in February or March, while they generally begin in August or September in the northern hemisphere. Keep those dates in mind if you want to experience grape-picking, which is physically difficult work but obviously important; it would be better to arrive early rather than too late.

* If possible, try to be available for at least two weeks or up to one month. This length of time allows you to develop skills that will make you more useful. Additionally, you can pick up some of the local language, meet other producers in the area, and ideally befriend your winemaker host and build a long-lasting relationship.

* In terms of compensation, always check the country's labor laws and

secure the correct visa for your circumstances. However, you could also volunteer, in which case you may hope to share wine-soaked meals with the harvest team and winemaker as thanks for your efforts.

* Be conscious about documenting your harvest experience on social media; ask the winemaker if it's okay to take photos or videos, and be aware that this slows down your work pace. If you know that you're working quickly to fill the press before sundown, it's not the time to make a TikTok.

* Arrive prepared. Bring jeans, overalls, leather or waterproof slip-on boots, gloves, any medications you need, a refillable water bottle, and a can-do attitude, as well as a sense of awareness of what's happening around you. It's common for interns to injure themselves right at the start of harvest, so calm your excitement right down when you get there, and do your work methodically and with care. And be sure to get travel insurance.

# VISITS & TASTINGS: ETIQUETTE & A FORM FOR TAKING NOTES

**The chance to visit the natural winemaker of your dreams doesn't come often, so when you've finally set up the appointment (via your friend of a friend who knows their importer), brushed up on your Duolingo skills, flown to France, rented a car, driven two hours, and finally located the winery, you will want to be prepared so as to get the most out of the visit.**

It's important to understand that the great majority of natural winemakers do not have a public tasting room—like the ones you see in Napa Valley—to receive you. Instead, you'll be entering their production site and personal space, perhaps even having a homemade meal on their kitchen patio. Because of the personal nature of natural winemaking, most producers do not accept visits from the general public—hence the need for some kind of personal connection. If you don't have one, try writing an email explaining your passion for their wines. Be very specific about your reason for visiting; if it's simply to appreciate and learn, that's fine, but be clear about it so they know you don't have any commercial intentions. Ask if there will be a fee for the visit and how it can be paid. If there is no fee, the appropriate thing to do is bring a small gift from your home town, and offer to purchase wine with cash. A bar of artisanal dark chocolate, a jar of jam, or whatever you can bring on the journey is a simple but meaningful gesture, while purchasing a bottle of wine with cash is a way to pay for your visit.

During your time at the winery, you'll likely be shown the winery itself, as well as a vineyard if it's close by. We all live in a world of smartphones, and it's understandable that you will be snapping pics with your device, but if your head is constantly bent toward a screen, you remove yourself from any chance of cultural exchange, especially if there's a language barrier. Also, it's kind of rude: This person is taking time out of a busy day to show you around, and you're not present. To avoid this, instead of taking notes on your phone or obsessively photographing, make a scan of the form below, and bring printouts. Keep your visit notes in a folder someplace, or make a book of them. You can even cut out photos and glue them onto the page, like the scrapbooks we made as kids.

One last bit of etiquette: Send a thank-you. It can be a handwritten, air-mailed card, or simply a message on Instagram with a photo of you enjoying their wines at your local watering hole. Either way, it demonstrates your appreciation and also gives them a chance to remember who you are and to stay in touch if they'd like.

# NATURAL WINE VISIT

DATE:

___

TOWN, REGION, COUNTRY:

___

WINERY NAME:

___

PRODUCER(S) FIRST & LAST NAME(S):

___

WINERY OVERVIEW & HISTORY:

___

SOIL TYPES:

___

VINEYARD FARMING PRACTICES & HISTORY:

___

WINE 1:
CUVÉE NAME:
VINTAGE:
EXPLANATION:
TASTING NOTES:


WINE 2:
CUVÉE NAME:
VINTAGE:
EXPLANATION:
TASTING NOTES:


WINE 3:
CUVÉE NAME:
VINTAGE:
EXPLANATION:
TASTING NOTES:


WINE 4:
CUVÉE NAME:
VINTAGE:
EXPLANATION:
TASTING NOTES:


WINE 5:
CUVÉE NAME:
VINTAGE:
EXPLANATION:
TASTING NOTES:

## MEAL OR BITES PAIRED WITH WINES:

_____

_____

_____

## FAVORITE WINE:

_____

_____

_____

## THINGS TO RESEARCH:

_____

_____

_____

# OTHER NOTES, MAPS, & DOODLES

# GETTING INTO A NATURAL WINE CAREER

## WITH REBEKAH PINEDA, SALES MANAGER AT C. CASSIS, NEW YORK

So, now you've got the bug, and while you can't even imagine what it's like to devote yourself to natural wine professionally, you feel the calling.

Think about how you can apply your background to this new field—if you worked in tech, marketing, education, whatever it is, it will be relevant. Wine is multifaceted, and literally every professional skill imaginable applies to something in its supply chain.

Your goal is to learn as much as possible in your first few wine-industry jobs, and there are two ideal positions for this: One is wine-store retail, and the other is in a winery. Once you've worked in either of those, you will have so much inside knowledge that you will be able to work in a larger wine business, such as an importer.

Natural wine industry pro Rebekah Pineda—currently the sales manager at C. Cassis, a fermented fruit-drink project in New York's Hudson Valley—was previously part of the team at natural wine shop Domestique in Washington, DC. Here she shares some reflections on her first forays into this career and what she advises for those thinking of diving in.

**IN YOUR FIRST NATURAL WINE JOB, WHAT WAS THE ROLE, AND WHAT WERE YOUR MAIN TAKEAWAYS ABOUT NATURAL WINE?**

My first job in the natural wine world was helping open Domestique. Before that, I worked at places like [wine distributor] Weygandt-Metzler and several restaurants, but none of them really identified as part of the natural wine scene. I'm a big reader and researcher, so working at the shop was the perfect chance to take all that online knowledge and actually put it into practice—meeting importers, winemakers, and even traveling to France. As a buyer, I also got to taste a lot, which was amazing. It was all about connecting what I read with what I experienced in real life.

I loved my time at Domestique—it was a period of incredible growth, both professionally and personally. Now, after living in New York City for more than five years, I can't help but wish we had focused less on France and more on Americana (wines and culture) in the beginning. The natural wine world is so heavily shaped by places like Paris, New York, and Oakland, and it creates an imbalance in how restaurants, shops, and tastes evolve. I believe the focus should shift, embracing a broader, more diverse narrative beyond these few epicenters.

**WHAT ADVICE WOULD YOU GIVE TO SOMEONE WHO IS IN THEIR MID-20S OR OLDER WHO WANTS TO WORK IN THE NATURAL WINE WORLD? WHERE DO THEY START? WHAT IS THE ONE THING THEY NEED TO FIND OR DO IN ORDER TO LEARN, EXPERIENCE, EXPLORE, AND IDENTIFY THEIR PLACE?**

Start by finding a place with passionate owners who are hands-on every day. For me, it's never been about fancy titles—what you'll learn from experienced mentors is invaluable. Surround yourself with curious, dedicated people. Don't be afraid to start in unexpected places—working with [chef-restaurateur] Brooks Headley as he reopened Superiority Burger [in New York] taught me more about passion and focus than any wine role. In this industry, there's hustle—and then there's hustle with purpose. For me, the latter is the most rewarding.

# surround yourself with curious, dedicated people

# EXPERT VIEW: "OOPS, I BECAME A WINEMAKER"
## WITH ALANNA LAGAMBA OF FRAUENPOWER

Life isn't linear; sometimes, a circuitous path can lead us to a career or location we never anticipated. Sometimes, it makes us a natural winemaker.

Toronto native Alanna LaGamba was living in Berlin when she happened to meet an intriguing winemaker named Martin Wörner from Germany's Rheinhessen region, a six-and-a-half-hour drive from the capital. Martin was showing the first release of his label Marto, made from vineyards his family had been farming for generations. Intrigued by the wines—as well as by their maker—and craving some time away from Berlin, where she was working at the natural wine bar Jaja, Alanna headed south to join Martin for a week of vineyard work. That week turned into the whole harvest season and, eventually, to becoming life partners and winemakers together in the Marto label—with Alanna's distinctive sparkling wine Frauenpower making waves around the world.

Unlike people born into a winemaking family, Alanna had to find her own way and her own voice in the small town of Flonheim, where Marto is based. Her story reveals how natural winemaking is founded largely on individual style and intuition. It also serves as a cautionary tale: That harvest experience may lead to a lifetime of adventures in fermentation.

**WHAT'S THE STORY BEHIND FRAUENPOWER, WHICH TRANSLATES TO "WOMEN POWER"?**
In my first vintage, 2019, I'd been living [in Flonheim], and it felt like… I really love what we're doing, but let's say I spend the rest of my life here, I don't want it to be someone else's project. So, I said I'd like to do something of my own, and Martin asked, "What grape do you want?" I said Pinot Noir, and he said, "How about Dornfelder?" We had almost no Pinot Noir at the time.

I'm half Italian, and when I was in university I worked at this Italian place, and we always drank Lambrusco. There's something I always liked about it, but I didn't like that it was kind of sweet. So, I said, "Why don't we make a Lambrusco-style?"

Dornfelder was planted in the 1980s all over the Rheinhessen. The color is really dark. After two days of

maceration, it's pitch black. It never really gets above 10 degrees alcohol; it's high yielding, but it doesn't really get high sugar. It's like the Prosecco grape [Glera]: On its own, it's not very exciting, but when you add bubbles it elevates it and makes it fruity and refreshing. That's how Frauenpower was born.

**YOUR FIRST WINE EVER WAS A PÉT-NAT. THAT'S AN INTIMIDATING PLACE TO START, ISN'T IT?**
That first year, Frauenpower was really explosive. If you have a white kitchen, like, ciao. We were wondering is there gonna be a second year? Then we found a way that works for us so that it's not as explosive.

Winemaking's not like cooking, where if you mess up a recipe you can try again the next day. You have one shot per year. But the longer you do it, the more you learn.

Now, we have these massive 15,000-liter tanks that are lengthwise, so now we use them for the pét-nat—because with the length, the wine settles really well—and then we rack multiple times so that there's less sediment. My dad always says, "If you learn from it, that's only half a mistake." I apply that logic to winemaking; especially when you are working without sulfur, there will always be errors.

**HOW HAVE YOU NAVIGATED WINEMAKING WITHOUT HAVING ANY FORMAL TRAINING?**
Working at Jaja, co-owner Etienne Dodet was my mentor; he really shaped my palate. He'd be, like, "Oh, try this"—and most of the wines were sulfur-free.

I think when you come from [a non-producer background], your mind is freer and you can think more out of the box. For the first few years, Martin and I were harvesting Pinot at 10 degrees [alcohol]. Martin—who studied winemaking at Geisenheim University [renowned for its enology program]—wanted "freshness" and thought harvesting it too ripe would make it slow and alcoholic. We'd try Pinots that were much riper yet still super-fresh, and I said, "Why are we harvesting at 10 degrees?" Now we

# "if you learn from it that's only half a mistake"

realize you can harvest Pinot super-ripe because [our region is] cool-climate, and you still have freshness [as in, acidity].

**YOU'RE FROM TORONTO AND LIVED IN BERLIN, BUT NOW YOU LIVE IN A SMALL GERMAN VILLAGE. HAS THAT BEEN AN ADJUSTMENT?**
I cannot stress more how much I never wanted to live in the countryside. I'm a city person. When I first moved here, it was not an easy adjustment. I didn't speak German. I didn't have my driver's license. I used to walk 10km [6 miles] to get my hair cut just to have independence, or bike to get sourdough bread 30km [18 miles] away.

Now I speak German and have a German passport. I think as humans we're easily adaptable, and now I really love living here—to the point where I can't even imagine living anywhere else. I'm a runner, and often when I do my running routes through the vines, I'm looking around, thinking, it's so beautiful. I really love vineyard work. And I like that there's constant change—you're never doing the same thing.

**WHAT'S YOUR ADVICE FOR PEOPLE WHO FEEL THE URGE TO MAKE NATURAL WINE?**
Nothing is ever what you think it will be—embrace it. I used to come up with ideas of what we might do in harvest, and Martin was, like, "You can't plan anything, you have to go with the flow. You have to be adaptable." It's made me, in a way, much calmer, because there are so many things I can't control. Don't be afraid of the unexpected, because it will come a lot. And don't be afraid of setbacks, because they will happen.

# OH, THE WINE-SOAKED PLACES YOU'LL GO

**NO TWO NATURAL WINES ARE THE SAME. Even within the same barrel, differences will emerge in a bottling. Similarly, no two natural wine journeys are the same. Yours is yours, and it will include experiences, mistakes, and lessons that are yours alone. From here, you'll continue exploring the genre, and meanwhile it will keep changing and introducing new characters.**

Natural wine has a significant role in the world. By choosing to support vineyards that farm without chemicals and that focus on the wellbeing of their entire ecosystem—including soil, animals, insects, and workers, as well as the end consumer—not only do we make a small difference while climate change is rapidly advancing, but we also keep vineyard heritage and biodiversity alive.

Ultimately, natural wine is consumable culture: When you put a bottle on the table, you invite conversation. And the best thing is, each bottle inspires an entirely new set of questions, stories, and so much more.

# FURTHER READING

Now that you've got the natural wine bug, here are just a few resources to deepen your knowledge:

## BOOKS

*Natural Trailblazers*, by Camilla Gjerde (2025)
Swedish writer Camilla Gjerde self-published this collection of profiles, of 13 visionaries of natural wine who are thinking about a "low-carbon future" while they grow and vinify wine. Find it on her website: camillagjerde.com.

*Natural Wine, No Drama,* by Honey Spencer (Pavilion Books, 2024)
Honey Spencer is a London-based sommelier and co-owner of Sune restaurant. This book leverages Honey's extensive hospitality experience and deep connections within the natural wine world, to explain its intricacies in approachable language.

*The World of Natural Wine*, by Aaron Ayscough (Artisan, 2022)
Paris-based writer Aaron Ayscough has long covered the world of natural wine from a French perspective through his blog-turned-newsletter, "Not Drinking Poison in Paris." This book details every aspect of natural wine including numerous profiles of mostly French producers.

*Amber Revolution*, by Simon Woolf (Interlink Books, 2018)
Leading the way on the orange wine craze is writer Simon Woolf, who has long been entrenched in the Italy-Slovenia nexus, Georgia, and elsewhere. In this book, he investigates the history and making of skin-contact white wines, with emphasis on organic and natural wine.

*Wine Pairing for the People*, by Cha McCoy (Harvest, 2025)
Sommelier Cha McCoy brings together cooking and wine with this tome devoted to non-European cuisines, offering her expert advice on what to pair with recipes that feature spice and tang.

*Poetry is Growing in Our Garden*, by Anders Frederik Steen (Apartamento Publishing, 2021)
From 2013–2020, Ardèche-based natural winemaker Anders Frederik Steen kept a detailed journal chronicling his passion for natural wine, eventually including his first vintages. It's an indispensable glimpse into the mindset of a producer.

*Champagne*, by Peter Liem (Mitchell Beazley, 2017)
To delve further into the world of Champagne, I recommend reading wine writer Peter Liem's website or his hefty book on Champagne, as well as a week-long trip to the region.

## MAGAZINES

*Pipette Magazine*, worldwide
In 2017, I founded *Pipette Magazine* as the world's first print magazine devoted to natural wines. Issues 8-9-10 remain available on the Pipette website, with worldwide shipping: pipettemagazine.com.

*Swurl*, New York
This digital media brand devoted to wine and education offers helpful explainers and recommendations on their Instagram page, @swurl.media.

## RAISIN: THE APP FOR NATURAL WINE LOVERS

Originally French but now global, with offerings in several languages, Raisin is an indispensable website and app for finding natural wines anywhere in the world. I have used it on nearly every single road trip to discover restaurants and bottle shops where I might quench my thirst, naturally.

Raisin offers location-based listings of venues that sell natural wines—they must have a minimum of 30 percent natural wines to be included—as well as wineries that operate this way. You can also learn about upcoming natural wine fairs and events, and read helpful blog posts and articles on the site. Users upload photos and descriptions of natural wines they've recently enjoyed, too. Available in English, French, Italian, and Japanese, Raisin is helmed by hardworking, passionate volunteers, so occasionally things aren't totally up to date, but it's a wealth of information.

# INDEX

**A**

aging 93, 146–7
    lees aging 92–3
amphorae 13, 25, 26
anthroposophy 39, 75
AOC (*appellations d'origine contrôlée*) 64–5
Armani, Giulio 46
Artigas, Oriol 37
artisanal wines 66
Augusta, Turin 191
Australian Wine Research Institute 111

**B**

Barraco, Nino 48
Beau Paysage 59
Beaujolais 19–20
Beck, Judith 119
Bichi Wines 55
Binner, Christian 39
biodynamic farming 17, 35, 38–40, 75–7
    biodynamic calendar 78–9
    Gut Oggau 119–20
blends 33
bottling 95
Bouvot, Alice 40
*Brettanomyces* 135, 138
brightness 132
Brumaire, California 191
bubbles 107–8, 163
    Costadilà Móz 163
    Danger 380 Volts 162

Moussamoussettes 163
Oyster River Morphos 163–4
The Other Right Bright Young Thing 164
butternut squash soup 167–8

**C**

C. Cassis, New York 205
Cannizzo, Gianluca 191
Cantina Giardino 50
carbo-crema with rigatoni alla villana 171–2
carbon sequestration 23, 75
carbonic maceration 88–9
careers in wine 205–6
Champagne 13, 35, 107
Champagne Benoît Lahaye 38
chaos theory 119–20
chaptalization 19, 87
Chardonnay 101
Charmat method 31, 107
Chauvet, Jules 19–20
cheese platter 175
Chenin Blanc 40, 42
cleaning 94
*col fondo* 31
cork taint (TCA) 139
crushing grapes 86
cuttings 103
*cuvée* 40

**D**

De Gruttola, Daniela 50
decanting 145
Denavolo 46
describing wine 131–2
    bright or lively 132
    fruity 132
    funky 135
    mineral 135
    tannic 132–5
dessert 179
Di Gruttola, Antonio 50
dinner parties 159, 180
    course recipes 167–8, 171–2, 175, 179
    glassware & set-up 159
    making wine memories 183
    pure bubbles 163–4
    welcome drinks 161
disgorgement 30, 108
DOC 64–5
Dodet, Etienne 210
Domaine Binner 39
Domaine de l'Ange Vin 40
Domaine de l'Octavin 40
Domaine Mosse 42, 163
Domestique, Washington, DC. 205–6
*dosage* 35, 38, 157

**E**

ethyl acetate (EA) 86, 136
Europe 64–5, 187

**F**
fermentation 86–7, 101
　primary & malolactic fermentations 90–1
　re-fermentation 138
fermented dry 30
filtration 92–3
fining 66, 92
flaws 136
　*Brettanomyces* 138
　cork taint (TCA) 139
　ethyl acetate (EA) 136
　mousiness 136
　oxidation 137
　re-fermentation 138
　reduction 137
　volatile acidity (VA) 136
　what to do if a wine is flawed 140–1
Food and Agricultural Organization (FAO) 23
food pairing 149–53
　butternut squash soup 167–8
　carbo-crema with rigatoni alla villana 171–2
　cheese platter 175
　dessert 179
　food pairings to avoid 156–7
　food pairings to try 155
Foradori, Elisabetta 46
Foster, Anika and Chris 61–3
Frauenpower 62, 208–11
Freya, Ének 26

fruitiness 132
fungicides 74
funkiness 135

**G**
Gamay 19, 33
Ganevat, Anne & Jean-François 38
Gang of Four 20, 68
Georgia, Republic of 25–6
glassware 159
Glera 31
*glou glou* 32, 61–2, 88
glyphosate 74
grafting 103
Grower Champagne 35
Guniava, Archil and Nino 26
Gut Oggau 119–20

**H**
H2O Vegetal, Tarragona, Spain 192
harvesting grapes 81–2
　experiencing 194–7
Hawkins, Craig and Carla 59
Headley, Brooks 206
Heekin, Deirdre 56
heirloom grape varieties 102–3
herbicides 74
Houillon, Emmanuel 43

**I**
Iago's Wine 26

**J**
Jaja, Berlin 208, 210
Julie Restaurant, Melbourne 149–53
Jura wines 63

**K**
Karakterre, Austria and New York 191
Kull, Simone and Joy 171

**L**
La Dive Bouteille, Loire Valley 190
La Garagista 56
labels 126
　alcohol content 127
　*appellation* 127
　certification 128
　*cuvée* name 126–7
　grape variety 127
　importer 128
　pregnancy warning 128
　producer name 126
　region 127
　sulfites 128
　vintage 127
　volume 128
LaGamba, Alanna 62, 208–11
Lapierre, Marcel 20
Laval, Vincent 189
lees 31
　lees aging 92–3
Legeron, Isabelle 190
liveliness 132
Louis Roederer 35
Lubbe, Tom 42

Lucy M Wines 59
Lynch, Kermit 20

**M**
maceration 85
    carbonic maceration 88–9
    macerated white wine 28, 85
Maine Wild Wine Fest, Freeport, Maine 192
Maison Pierre Overnoy 43
malolactic fermentation 90–1
Marie-Courtin 35
Martens, Anna 50
Marto 61, 208
massal selection 103
Matassa 42
Meinklang 62
Milan Nestarec 53, 163
minerality 135
MORE Natural Wine 61–3
mousiness 136, 141

**N**
Narioo, Eric 50
natural wine 13–14, 213
    careers 205–6, 208–11
    defining 17
    exploring 125
    natural wine bars 187
    natural wine fairs 189–92
    rising popularity 22–3
    talking about it 68–9
    vegan concerns 66

natural winemaking 77, 81
    bottling 95
    carbonic maceration 88–9
    cleaning 94
    crushing grapes 86
    fermentation, punch-downs, & pump-overs 86–7
    filtration, racking & lees aging 92–3
    harvesting 81–2
    pressing 91
    primary & malolactic fermentations 90–1
    settling & aging 93
    sorting 82
    stages of natural vinification 96–9
    stems, skins & orange wine 82–6
    styles 28–35
Néauport, Jacques 19–20
négociant 38
non-industrial farming 77

**O**
O'Kane, Sophie 149–53
Occhipinti 51
Okamoto, Eishi 59
Orange Glou Fair, New York 192
orange white wine 28, 85
organic farming 17, 19–20, 23, 35, 73, 77
    conventional farming triad 74
*ouillé* 43

Overnoy, Pierre 43, 63
oxidation 137

**P**
Pācina 48
Partida Creus 37
pesticides 74
pét-nat (*pétillant-naturel*) wine 30, 107–8
    pét-nat spritz 161
Pheasant's Tears 26, 55
*pied de cuve* 87
Pineau d'Aunis 40
Pineda, Rebekah 205–6
Pinto Gris 33
piquette 32
Planck, Max 119
Pliny the Elder 114
polyculture 104
Preisinger, Claus 61–2, 119
pressing grapes 91
primary fermentation 90–1
producers 36
    Americas 55–6
    Australia 59
    Austria 45
    Czechia 53
    France 38–43
    Georgia 55
    Germany 44
    Italy 46–51
    Japan 59
    South Africa 59
    Spain 37
Prosecco 31, 107
pump-overs 86–7
punch-downs 86–7
Pura Sede, Lisbon 192

## Q
*quevri* 25–6, 55

## R
racking 92–3
Radikon 53
Raw Wine fairs 190–1
re-fermentation 138
reduction 137
refermented-in-bottle 31
regenerative agriculture 75
Robinot, Pierre 40
rootstock 103
Roundup 74
Ruppert-Leroy 35
Ruth Lewandowski 56

## S
Salon St-Jean, Loire Valley 190
Schulkin, Alex 111–13, 164
Seethiah, Nagesh 149–50
serving temperatures 143–5
settling 93
Shobbrook, Jauma and Tom 59
Signer, Rachel 59
single-variety wines 59
skin-contact white wine 28, 85
Solo Uva, Linguaglossa, Sicily 192
*Somm* 131
sorting grapes 82
sparkling wines 107–8, 163–4
Steiner, Rudolf 39, 75, 78
stems and skins 82–6

Strohmeier, Franz 45
sulfites 17, 19, 33, 111–13

## T
tannins 132–5
tasting wine 131–2
    potential flaws 136–9
*terroir* 114–15, 135
Testalonga 59
The Wild Bunch, Portland, Oregon 192
Third Coast Soif, Chicago, Illinois 192
Thun, Maria 78–9
travel 187
    harvest experiences 194–7
    natural wine bars 187
    natural wine fairs 189–92
    visits & tastings 199–203
Trossen, Rita & Rudolf 44
Tscheppe, Eduard and Stephanie 119
Tschida, Christian 45, 119

## U
ullage 43

## V
Van Klopper, Anton 59
varietal wines 59
vegan concerns 66
*vin nature* 68–9
vine-growing 102
    grafting 103

heirloom grape varieties 102–3
    massal selection 103
    polyculture 104
Vino di Anna 50
visiting winemakers 199
    etiquette 199
    record-keeping 200–3
*Vitis vinifera* 13, 25, 56
volatile acidity (VA) 82, 86, 101, 135, 136, 141

## W
Waters, Alice 20
whole-bunch 46
wine bars 187
    Asia & Oceania 187
    Europe 187
    US & Canada 187
wine fairs 189–92
wine shopping 125
    decoding wine labels 126–8
Winkler, Doreen 192
Woolf, Simon 69
World Health Organization 74
Wörner, Martin 208–11
WSET (Wine & Spirit Education Trust) 125
Wurdeman, John 55

## Z
Zero Compromise, Tsibilisi 192

# ABOUT THE AUTHOR

Originally from the USA, Rachel Signer is the author of Y*ou Had Me at Pét-Nat: A Natural Wine-Soaked Memoir*, named by *The New York Times* as one of 2021's best wine books. She is the founder and publisher of cult natural wine magazine *Pipette Magazine*, distributed in 30 countries.

Based in Australia, where she has also made natural wine for six years, Signer leads boutique natural wine tours in Italy and regularly teaches food-and-drink-writing workshops. Follow on Instagram @rachsig and @pipettemagazine.

# ACKNOWLEDGMENTS

This book was written largely on the traditional lands of the Peramangk and Kaurna people. I acknowledge and pay my respects to the past, present, and future Traditional Owners and Custodians of Country throughout so-called Australia, and extend this acknowledgement and respect to Traditional Owners across the world.

Thank you to the numerous winemakers and wine professionals who have taken the time to chat with me and welcomed me into their spaces to share their dedication and craft—whether directly for this book or for general knowledge over the years. This generosity is much appreciated.

Thank you to the wonderful team at Mitchell Beazley, in particular my editor, Jeannie Stanley, and the art director for this book, Ben Gardiner; to all the photographers whose work appears within, particularly Laura Scherb, who accompanied me on winery visits in central Italy; to Angelo Dolojan for the illustrations; and to my agent, Laura Nolan.

Thank you to my husband, Anton, for the conversation, the wine, and the support.

A heartfelt thank you to everyone who has shared wine or words with me over the years. You are all part of this book.

First published in Great Britain in 2026 by Mitchell Beazley, an imprint of Octopus Publishing Group Ltd
Carmelite House
50 Victoria Embankment
London EC4Y 0DZ
www.octopusbooks.co.uk

An Hachette UK Company
www.hachette.co.uk

The authorized representative in the EEA is Hachette Ireland, 8 Castlecourt Centre, Dublin 15, D15 XTP3, Ireland (email: info@hbgi.ie)

Text copyright © Rachel Signer 2026
Design and layout copyright ©
Octopus Publishing Group 2026
Illustrations copyright © Angelo Dolojan 2026

Distributed in the US by Hachette Book Group, 1290 Avenue of the Americas, 4th and 5th Floors, New York, NY 10104

Distributed in Canada by Canadian Manda Group, 664 Annette St., Toronto, Ontario, Canada M6S 2C8

All rights reserved. No part of this work may be reproduced or utilized in any form or by any means, electronic or mechanical, including photocopying, recording or by any information storage and retrieval system, without the prior written permission of the publisher.

Rachel Signer asserts the moral right to be identified as the author of this work.

ISBN: 978-1-84091-981-3
eISBN: 978-1-84091-982-0

A CIP catalogue record for this book is available from the British Library.

Printed and bound in China.

10 9 8 7 6 5 4 3 2 1

Commissioning Editor: Jeannie Stanley
Art Director: Ben Gardiner
Editor: Scarlet Furness
Copy Editor: David Tombesi-Walton
Food Stylist: Emma Cantlay
Prop Stylist: Louie Waller
Picture Research Manager: Jen Veall
Assistant Production Manager: Allison Gonsalves

Photographers: Kim Lightbody, Laura Scherb, and Rachel Signer

Cover illustration + illustrations on pp. 21, 67, 68, 89, 96–99, 102, 103, 104, 126, 129, 137, 140, 144, 154, 156 and 204: Angelo Dolojan

Photography credits: Courtesy Agricola Foradori. Photo: Emanuele Camerini: 47; Carmen Alcedo: 223; © Leila Ashtari: 48; Cephas Picture Library: © Jean-Bernard Nadeau 75; Domaine Christian Binner: 39; © Suzan Gabrijan: 52; Michael Gardenia: 15; Kim Lightbody: 9, 16, 19, 25, 29, 30, 31, 32, 33, 34, 37r, 38, 40, 41, 42, 45, 50, 51, 53, 54, 55, 57, 58, 59, 80, 107, 109, 124, 130, 133, 134, 142, 160, 162, 165, 166, 169, 170, 173, 174, 176–177, 178, 179, 180, 182, 207, 210, 214-215; © Sofia Lisi: 100; MORE Natural Wine: 43, 60, 209; © Michael Persico: 22; Lewis Potter: 198; Linsey Rendell 26-27; Ruth Lewandowski Wines/ Photographer Cayce Clifford: 56; Laura Scherb: 12, 49, 72, 76, 84, 105, 114, 116-117, 158, 186, 212; © Barbara Schmidt-Keller 44; © Diletta Sereni: 46; Rachel Signer: 36, 37l, 64, 83, 87, 90, 95, 110, 118, 121, 148, 150, 152, 194, 195, 197; © Ania Smelskaya: 188, 193.